MW00424738

NOTHING TO APOLOGIZE FOR The Truth About Western Civilization

DONNA CAROL VOSS

VANTAGES BOOKS, LLC
Kaysville, UT 84037
Copyright © 2017 by Donna Carol Voss

Cover designed by Gwyn Kennedy Snider

print: 978-0-9906226-7-3
epub: 978-0-9906226-6-6
mobi: 978-0-9906226-5-9

Manufactured in the United States of America

www.vantagesbooks.com

Yet, as it has been said, the purpose of studying history
is not to deride human action, nor to weep over it or to hate it,
but to understand it. And hopefully then to learn from it
as we contemplate our future.

— NELSON MANDELA

ALSO BY DONNA CAROL VOSS

Deep Dive: Sanctuary Cities
(co-authored with Brian Peyton Joyner)

*Hail to the Chief! 10 Questions to Ask
Every Oval Office Candidate*

One of Everything: A Memoir

CONTENTS

Hey Hey, Ho Ho, Western Culture, Please Don't Go

On a cool and breezy day at Stanford in January 1987—Martin Luther King's birthday—the Reverend Jesse Jackson told a capacity crowd, "All of us, red, yellow, brown, black and white are precious in God's light and every human being is somebody worth respect and fellowship and a chance."

Well, who could disagree with that? In 1987, plenty of people, apparently. Not bad people, just people who didn't know better. Like Maya Angelou said, "You do what you know. When you know better, you do better." When we learned there was more culture than Western culture, we did better. But we also started to do worse.

It is the stuff of legend that after his speech, Jackson led 500 students to the Law School chanting, "Hey, Hey, Ho, Ho, Western culture has got to go." The truth, as it usually is, is much more interesting. An eyewitness to the event, a "lonely one-man truth squad," has been trying to correct the record ever since.[1] The students were chanting, yes, but Jackson was not. According to the eyewitness, when Jackson heard what the students were chanting, he said, "No, we don't want to get rid of Western culture. We want to expand it and bring in new voices." If only we had listened.

Western culture had been go, go, going for a while, but after that day at Stanford, it really went, went, went. It was such a heady realization that there was more to literature and history than what white, European males had given us. Unfortunately, in our zeal to include women, minorities, and non-Western cultures, we went a little overboard. We failed to heed the wise words of Reverend Jackson, which I'm paraphrasing as, "Don't throw the Western baby out with the bathwater."

Regrettably, we didn't just throw the baby out with the bathwater, we cursed its very existence. We pursued a scorched earth policy where nothing white, male, and European was allowed to hold its head up. We definitely needed to acknowledge our sins and right our wrongs, but the mistake we made was demonizing ourselves in the process.

We only became aware of our sins and wrongs because a hallmark of Western culture is its capacity to stimulate intellectual and moral progress. In proper context, the West's inexorable progress in moral and civil rights is remarkable. The rightful attainment of moral and civil rights by all groups in our society is such a given, we take it for granted. Without proper context, we blame Western culture for *creating* racism, sexism, homophobia, and all the other ills.

Without knowledge of the grand, sweeping arc of our history, we find ourselves defined by the evil of slavery. Without evaluation of Western culture in reference to other cultures, we hate ourselves for sexism and homophobia. Without historical appreciation for the power of capitalism to lift human societies out of abject poverty, its inherent greed and inequality become the only story.

Were we to teach them in context, women's suffrage and the Civil Rights Movement would induce pride in our unique American brand of Western culture. They would inculcate in us a deep appreciation

NOTHING TO APOLOGIZE FOR: THE TRUTH ABOUT WESTERN CIVILIZATION

for our brilliant system of government, which allows political protest, Constitutional amendments, and civil disobedience to achieve such progress. Without context, we find ourselves living in a perpetual Victim Olympics where members of previously harmed groups jockey for power; the more harmed the more power.

Yes, we in the West practiced the sickening atrocity of slavery for 300 years. Why didn't we continue to practice it for millennia as did the rest of the world? Because of the Enlightenment, that moment in the history of the West that transformed medieval world to modern world. Hierarchical political and social orders—monarchy, privileges accorded only the nobility, power and absolute authority of the Catholic Church—were replaced with values founded in human reason: freedom and equality for all.

Enlightenment thinkers in the 17th and 18th centuries employed reason to contemplate God, nature, and humanity, which led to the French and American Revolutions. Freedom, equality, and human reason also exposed slavery as a gross violation of the rights of man. It was the West that first abolished slavery: Britain in 1807; France in 1848; the United States in 1862. In the East, slavery continued well into the 20th century; the West African country of Mauritania did not abolish slavery until 1981.

Yes, Christianity was used to rationalize slavery as God's will, but it also served to elicit condemnation of slavery by Quakers and others for its un-Christian qualities.

Yes, women were second-class citizens for the first 100 plus years; we couldn't vote, own property, or sign contracts. We didn't have full civil rights until Title VII of the Civil Rights Act of 1964 barred discrimination on the basis of race, color, religion, sex, or national origin. Once those rights were attained, however, they were permanent.

When we compare ourselves to other cultures, Afghanistan for example, we see that moral and civil rights can just as easily go backward. Women in late 20th century Afghanistan enjoyed modern lives: education, independence, self-governance. When the Taliban came to power in 1996, women were made to veil themselves completely, ask permission to leave the home, and submit to sex with their husband at his whim with no right of refusal.

After the Taliban was ousted in 2001, Afghani women returned to "fragile but reversible" legal status,[2] which lasted only until US troops began withdrawing from Afghanistan in 2011. As the US withdrew, the Taliban resurged, and the Ministry of Justice banned family member testimony in criminal trials. Women are once again powerless to fight domestic violence and child and forced marriage.

Yes, sodomy was illegal in this country for a long time. Illinois was the first state to decriminalize sodomy in 1961, and not until 2003 did the Supreme Court rule that it is a violation of the Fourteenth Amendment to ban consensual sex between adults. Today, gay marriage is legal in all 50 states.

Iran, Saudi Arabia, and Syria today—today—punish men accused of homosexuality by beating them, lashing them, and/or throwing them to their death off building rooftops. ISIS arrogantly releases videos of same.

Yes, capitalism has created extreme disparity in wealth between the very rich and the very poor. It has also lifted more people out of poverty than any economic system in the world. In the socialist country of Venezuela—where everyone has free access to the same crappy healthcare—the people are so desperate for food they're butchering and eating flamingos, not to mention dogs, cats, donkeys, horses, and pigeons.[3]

Venezuela is sitting on the largest oil reserves in the world but can't extract and upgrade the heavy oil because it's too expensive. In the way that capitalism works best, Western companies invested billions of dollars in Venezuela's oil sector to unlock the reserves. As the price of Brent crude rose to $72/bbl in 2007, Venezuela's proven oil reserves increased, and it looked like the investment was going to pay off handsomely all around. Then, because Venezuela is socialist, the government expropriated the heavy oil investments.[4]

Instead of investing profits back into further development of the reserves—the most basic idea of Capitalism 101—the government siphoned money off for other things. Despite the significant rise in its recoverable oil post-Western investment, Venezuela's production of crude oil dropped 20 percent over the last decade. (During that same decade, US oil production rose more than 80 percent.) Venezuela still has a boatload of oil, but it is unrecoverable without outside investment, and you flunk Capitalism 101 if you burn your investors. Not only are ConocoPhillips and ExxonMobil out, so is every other Western oil company who saw what happened to them.[5]

Because socialism destroys economic freedom, confiscates private property, and controls price and currency, the people are eating dogs and cats they find in the street. Imagine a Venezuelan in your local Whole Foods or Costco, overwhelmed by its colorful profusion of fresh fruits and vegetables; its variety of fresh-baked breads and pastries; its cases full of different kinds of yogurt—regular, fat-free, Greek, probiotic, soy, frozen, fruit-on-the-bottom, blended. That's what capitalism can do. Why don't we teach that?

We don't teach that the universal rule of human society was poverty until capitalism came along. We don't teach that private enterprise and competition make life better. We don't teach that America is Western civilization's pearl of great price, a nation whose rights cannot be taken away because they're bestowed by our Creator. We don't teach that our American experiment is fragile and needs constant tending to preserve. We don't teach that, in context, America is something to be very, very proud of.

America is Western culture's highest expression and its last hope; we're the only ones left with much Western culture to speak of. Europe, which embraced a little too much multiculturalism a little too quickly, is trying desperately to put the genie back in its Western culture bottle, but its attempts are probably futile. When a culture is gone, it's gone.

We in this country are at a turning point. Do we unashamedly preserve what is best about Western culture? Or do we wring our hands and gulp *mea culpa* all the way to obliteration of the greatest country the world has ever known?

I love Western culture in America, and I am not ashamed. Let me make the case for it.

Back in the Day, Western Civ Was Cool

From the dawn of history until about 500 years before the birth of Christ, most people lived miserable, brutish lives in vast empires at the mercy of tyrannical rulers. Ancient empires in Mesopotamia, Egypt, China, Persia, and India were known for their opulent splendor, which splendor was exacted from peasants by confiscatory taxation, seizure of surplus production, and forced labor. Peasant families lived lives of abject poverty not much better than their animals.

Wonders of the ancient world, such as the Sphinx, the Hanging Gardens of Babylon, and the Taj Mahal, were possible because there was nothing so cheap as human life. It took millions of Chinese peasants to build the Grand Canal in China, and more than a million of them died from hunger or hard labor doing it.[6]

These were not people in the mood to play. They didn't have the luxury of self-reflection. Creativity and love of learning? Fahgettaboudit. There's a reason ancient Egyptians were so obsessed with death: they couldn't wait.

If there had been an ancient Greek Empire at the time, it might have been the same. But there wasn't. There was only the Greek people scattered throughout a thousand city-states in what is today Greece, Sicily, and Southern Italy. A multitude of mountain ranges and islands prevented Greeks from creating a vast empire controlled by a central capital. Instead they congregated on islands and in valleys between mountain ranges, which forced their city-states to remain small and—more importantly—independent.

"Unfavorable" geography, disunity, and competition were about to rock the world because disunity and competition are fundamental to modernity, which is requisite for Western civilization. Over nearly 300 years of modernity, Greeks brought forth democracy, philosophy, science, and reason. Oh, and games. The first people ever with the leisure to play gave us the Olympics.

Western civilization began with the Greeks.

The Unexamined Life Is Not Worth Living

If you had to give an "elevator pitch" for Western civilization, i.e., you had a person hostile to Western culture trapped in an elevator with you for 30 seconds, how could you sell it? Easy. "It gave the world freedom to think."

Think about that for a minute (fully drenched in the irony of thinking about thinking). Before the Greeks, thinking wasn't even on the radar. In Eastern civilization, the individual lived only to serve the state, and the state made things so miserable that the last thing the individual wanted to do was think. After all, what's the point of thinking if there's nothing you can do to change things? Instead, Eastern civilization prized escape from the intellect.

The unifying belief of Eastern religions and philosophical traditions was that the external world was an illusion to be overcome and only by doing so could one overcome suffering. Jainism prized non-attachment to possessions and celibacy(!). Taoism prized living in harmony with the natural course of things, i.e., no struggling, opposing or striving. Buddhism prized nirvana, the transcendent state of no suffering, desire, or sense of self.

Where the domain of the intellect did exist, as in Egypt, it belonged to the priests. The priesthood's power was tremendous; even pharaohs were subject to it. With power, of course, comes greed for more power, and the priests had no intention of letting the people think for themselves. Ignorance caused people to fear the whims of various gods and the absolutely terrifying magical forces they controlled. Ignorance kept the priestly Brahmans in the business of providing spiritual guidance to a frightened populace.

In the ancient world, chaos was believed to be the fundamental feature of the universe. As such, there was no point in seeking natural explanations for events. It never occurred to the Egyptians to investigate why the Nile flooded every year. Egypt's entire civilization depended on the Nile's annual flooding, yet they were content to attribute it to the tears of the goddess Isis crying for her dead husband Osiris.[7]

Into this world burst the Greeks and the brightness of their intellect. The Greeks taught themselves to reason, and the world is better for it. It's almost impossible to imagine the daring it took early Greeks to challenge the orthodoxy of a chaotic universe ruled by gods and magical forces. When Galileo challenged the geocentric theory of the universe more than 1600 years later, he stood on the shoulders of giants.

Science and God

The idea that science and God are antagonistic is just ignorant.[8] Scientific inquiry is only plausible with the doctrine of a rational creator of a rational universe. The Greeks were the first to propose an orderly universe governed by underlying principles that are *discernible by human reason.* Greeks invented the scientific method and all science goes back to them.

Unique to the Greeks was a determination to understand the natural world by observing outside facts and reasoning about them. Instead of accepting that diseases were the gods' way of punishing humans, early Greeks collected data and conducted experiments showing that disease was a natural process. Instead of using special magic rites to heal, which, for some strange reason, weren't very effective, Greek physicians used their knowledge of nature to identify the signs and symptoms of a body reacting to disease. The Greek physician Hippocrates is called the father of Western medicine, and the Hippocratic Oath is still the epitome of 21st century medical ethics: respect those who have passed down medical knowledge; teach that knowledge to the next generation; respect patients; and do no harm.

The Greeks were equally determined to understand mathematics, especially geometry. The Egyptians, Babylonians, and the Indus Valley Civilization were among the first to use geometric techniques as a matter of practical necessity, but they were uninterested in the rules that governed them. It was the Greeks who insisted that the rules and axioms governing geometry be established by deductive reasoning. The geometrical axioms and rules of Euclid, Pythagoras, and Archimedes are still taught today.

Early Greeks excelled at the systematic study of nature. Aristotle is called the father of zoology because he pioneered the observational and theoretical study of animals. Theophrastus, a student of Aristotle, is called the father of botany. The Greeks shattered prevailing assumptions in astronomy, biology, and physics. So much influence did they have on early concepts of science that most symbols used in physics and math today come from the Greek alphabet.

The Impact of Greek Thinking on Early Christianity

Two of the most influential thinkers and shapers of Western civilization are Plato and his student Aristotle. Plato's contributions to Western thought are legion, but his most valuable contribution was rational theology, i.e., the application of reason to expand understanding of religious questions and especially the nature of God. Through deductive reasoning, Plato concluded:

* The order in the universe cannot be explained without an intelligent cause, i.e., Divine Mind.
* God as Divine Mind is in every way perfect.
* God is immutable because were he to change, he could only become less perfect.
* There is one supreme god who is all-knowing, all-powerful and timeless.
* God is remote, impersonal and takes no part in anything.

Aristotle as well concluded that there must be a first cause of all motion and called that first cause God. Like Plato, he envisioned a rational but remote and impersonal god, who, having set the universe in motion, retired to contemplate his own perfection, taking no part in and having no awareness of the world. Aristotle's most valuable contribution was formal logic—rules for correct reasoning—that we can use to increasingly deepen our understanding of this rational god.

There is some debate as to whether Greeks influenced Jews or Jews influenced Greeks—mainly between Greeks and Jews since each insists they are the intellectual benefactor of the other—but the overlap between the Greek intellectual revolution and Jewish theology is unmistakable. To begin, with "Israel" means "struggle with God" in Hebrew, so Jews were definitely on board with the Greek call for valid reasoning about a rational god. Like Plato's god, the Jews' god was supreme, eternal and immutable. Unlike Plato's god, Yahweh is the loving Creator who is conscious of humankind, communicates with us, and intervenes in our affairs.

The Christian God—Jesus Christ—incorporated those aspects of divinity that both Greeks and Jews agreed on: supreme, immutable, all-knowing, all-powerful, timeless, and rational. The Christians agreed with the Jews about God's nature: he is a personal, loving God who involves himself with and intervenes in the affairs of humankind. Christians also embraced the Jewish millennial view of a coming golden age when the Messiah will reign in peace on earth.

Where there was disagreement between Greek philosophy and Christian doctrine, early Christian theologians used reason and logic to show how much more rational and satisfying were the Christian views. This emphasis on logical reasoning—very different from the mysticism and meditation of Eastern religions—became the defining hallmark of Christianity.

Christian theologians were well aware that philosophy is progressive. Socrates' learning surpassed that of his teachers, Plato's knowledge exceeded that of Socrates, and Aristotle's that of Plato. Christians elevated the use of reason well beyond that of the Greeks.

The faith in reason and progress embodied in Christianity underlies all of Western civilization.

The Impact of Christianity on Western Civilization
Western culture is defined by a fundamental belief in progress: the ability to reason our way forward to a better world. Only in

a world moving toward a brighter future does innovation make sense. There's a reason the West is known for its inventions and technologies: Penicillin, the Internet, the wheel-and-axle, the nail, the compass, the screw, the telephone, the internal combustion engine, the automobile, the waterwheel, the steam engine, the light bulb, the birth control pill, the printing press, the airplane, the space shuttle, the pacemaker, and indoor plumbing to name a few.

Ancient Eastern culture was defined by a fundamental belief in a timeless, cyclic universe where nothing can or should change: endless karmic cycling. Everything important to know was already known, and the concept of progress was factually wrong. Because timeless knowledge was the only knowledge that mattered, any accidental innovations tended to be ignored or isolated until they died out.

Dark Ages, Schmark Ages

It is pure, unadulterated hokum that Christianity killed Western progress after the fall of Rome. If you think the "Dark Ages" was a real thing, you're way behind the curve. Even Wikipedia says it isn't. So does The Columbia Encyclopedia, Britannica, and Rodney Stark in *How the West Won: The Neglected Story of the Triumph of Modernity*. The "Dark Ages" myth, according to Stark, was "made up by eighteenth-century intellectuals determined to slander Christianity and to celebrate their own sagacity."[9]

From the History Channel's *6 Reasons the Dark Ages Weren't So Dark*:[10]

Among the more popular myths about the "Dark Ages" is the idea that the medieval Christian church suppressed natural scientists, prohibiting procedures such as autopsies and dissections and basically halting all scientific progress. Historical evidence doesn't support this idea: Progress may have been slower in Western Europe during the Early Middle Ages, but it was steady, and it laid the foundations for future advances in the later medieval period.

Did Science and Learning Really Flourish Under Islam?

If you think science and learning flourished under Islam during the so-called "Dark Ages," you're still behind the curve, but you're in good company. This "myth" is trickier. The truth is that sophisticated Muslim culture originated with the cultures they conquered.

Recall that Mohammed and the "Rightly Guided Caliphs" began their conquest of the world in the 7th century.[11] It is widely believed that each conquered people was given the "choice" to convert to Islam or die. It makes much more sense, however, to accept the Islamic world's version of events: some may have been converted at the tip of a sword, but in most instances, the people were left to practice their own religion. In other words, the Muslim world spread; Islam did not.[12]

Why is that important? Because the so-called flourishing of Islam was really the continued flourishing of cultures conquered by Muslims. From that point forward, contributors to "Arab science" were given Arabic names and their works were published in the lingua franca of the Muslim world: Arabic. Ironically, it was the conquered people themselves who translated the contributions, but that in no way rendered the knowledge part of Arab culture.

A perfect example is Muhammad ibn Mūsā al-Khwārizmī, a "Muslim" mathematician known as the father of algebra. MuslimHeritage.com, whose mission is to "Discover the golden age of Muslim civilization," describes him thus:

"Muhammad ibn Musa Al-Khwarizmi is one of the greatest scientific minds of the medieval period and the most important Muslim mathematician, justly called the 'father of algebra'."[13]
In reality, al-Khwārizmī was a Persian (Zoroastrian) mathematician who converted to Islam as an adult.[14] The ruling Muslim Caliph of the Abbasid dynasty at that time, Harun al-Rashid, to his credit," brought culture to his court and tried to establish the intellectual disciplines which at that time were not flourishing in the Arabic world." Al-Rashid's son Al-Mamun continued his father's legacy and founded an academy called the House of Wisdom.

*He continued the patronage of learning started by his father and founded an academy called the House of Wisdom where Greek philosophical and scientific works were translated. He also built up a library of manuscripts, the first major library to be set up since that at Alexandria, collecting important works from Byzantium. In addition to the House of Wisdom, al-Mamun set up observatories in which **Muslim** astronomers could build on the knowledge acquired by earlier peoples.*[15]
[emphasis added]

Al-Khwārizmī was a scholar at the House of Wisdom where, in addition to translating Greek scientific manuscripts into Arabic, he studied and wrote on algebra, geometry, and astronomy. He used "Arabic" numerals (also referred to as Hindu-Arabic numerals), which were entirely of Indian origin, and the geometrical ideas of Euclid to develop algebra.[16]

The proof, if you will, that science and learning did not originate with Islam is the fact that science and learning disappeared as the original religions of Muslim conquered territories disappeared. By the fourteenth century, the so-called "Golden Age" of Islam was over.

My point here is not to throw Muslims under the bus but to throw light on why progress occurred in the West but not in the East. Progress simply wasn't (and isn't) possible under Islam where everything that happens is a direct result of Allah's will. To contemplate limits to Allah's power and authority—propose underlying rules of order—is blasphemy. Muslims did a phenomenal job of acquiring, translating and incorporating the knowledge of other cultures, but they made virtually no unique contribution to it. "A scientific culture was maintained within the Muslim lands, but little was done to advance it."[17]

The last great Islamic philosopher (emphasis on last) was Abū al-Walīd Muhammad ibn Ahmad ibn Muhammad ibn Rushd—called Averroës by Latin readers—born in 1126 at the far western edge (emphasis on western) of the Muslim world in Córdoba, Spain. As an influential religious judge and court physician, he had access to the writings of Aristotle (one of few Muslims who did). Averroës wrote a series of commentaries on Aristotle where he argued on behalf of philosophy. The commentaries were controversial because they promoted logic as the key to a true understanding of religion, a view widely regarded in Islam as heretical.[18]

Averroës himself acknowledged the danger that teaching philosophy to ordinary Muslims might undermine their confidence in Islam. He recommended it be taught only to a select few with great care. Is it any wonder that most of his works no longer survive in Arabic? Brilliant as he was, Averroës had very little influence on the Islamic world of his time. Where his commentaries *did* find rich soil—translated into Latin or Hebrew—was the Western world. Known throughout the great universities of Europe as "the Commentator," his commentaries were studied wherever Aristotle was studied all the way into the modern era.

The example of Averroës is a classic illustration of why the "Dark Ages-Golden Age" myth proves so durable. After the fall of Rome, the writings of Aristotle and others were lost to the Western world, which was subsequently deemed "backward" by future historians because it did not have access to the great Greek philosophers. It was the Muslim world that maintained Greek classics because of the persistence of Greek/Byzantine culture in conquered Arab societies. It is not incorrect to say Muslims "gave" Europeans Greek philosophy, but it is disingenuous to ignore that Greek philosophy never took hold in the Muslim world because of Islam.[19]

The reality is that Westerners, by dint of their belief in innovation and correction—progress—never stopped trying to understand and apply more of Aristotle's teachings. In the West, philosophy became a core ingredient (for a long time anyway) in any liberal education. It is the West that produced the scientific revolution despite our being far less advanced than ancient China and India at one point in time. Like China and India, everywhere on earth that scientific activity has flourished, it has inevitably declined—with one exception: the West is the single sustained success story of scientific flourishing.[20] (Say that five times fast.)

The Impact of Western Civilization on Political Power

Perhaps the most influential Greek experiment of all was democracy—*demos* (people) and *kratos* (power). From the dawn of time, people had existed for the sole purpose of being exploited by the aristocracy; no more powerful than ants on a hill. In 5th century Athens BC, direct democracy was born. All male citizens—wealthy landowners, artisans, shopkeepers, workers, and traders—shared equally in formal political power. No class distinctions existed between them, and all important issues were decided by majority vote.

Western civilization gave power to the people. It gave the world freedom to think. It gave us logic and reason and science and philosophy. It gave us a future brighter than today and the tools—reason and progress—for getting there. It gave us the means for moral progress and the ability to recognize the need for it.

Pause and let that sink in. Think about how people lived before the rise of the West. Think about Western culture's stunning achievements. Think about it all in context. Would you want it any other way?

Now that appreciation for Western civilization is solidly in our grasp, let's turn to its not-so-nice underbelly, which must also be understood in context.

Key Points
Western civilization:
- Was invented by the early Greeks (500 BC) before there was even a Greece.
- Freed people from being nothing but expendable resources to fulfill the whims of their rulers.
- Introduced reason, formal science, philosophy, the intellect, freedom, progress, democracy, and play.
- Gave the world the freedom and tools to think about it and ourselves.
- Gave us rational theology, i.e., a god that made sense, whose created universe made sense, which universe could be understood by the operation of natural laws.
- Is not a guarantee and largely disappeared when Rome went from republic to empire.

And:
- Rational theology was the basis of Christianity, which early Christians used to understand God and share the gospel.

- The Dark Ages are a myth; development was slower and less obvious after the fall of Rome, but many seeds were planted during that time for the Enlightenment, the Renaissance, and the Industrial Revolution.
- The so-called flourishing in the Islamic world was really continued flourishing of cultures that Muslims conquered.
- Our Founders drew heavily on Plato's ideas of democracy in the formation of our country.

Western Culture Is Messy,
I Can't Lie

Western civilization has given us great things, but it's not without dark underbelly, no question. The important point about dark underbelly is that it isn't unique to Western culture. Western culture has its own distinctly Western shade of yuck, but so does every other culture. Why? Because cultures are made up of people, and people can be awful.

Think about a sweet, innocent baby, free of racism, sexism, homophobia, and cruelty. Only nurture can build in the ugly part of the underbelly. But what infants (and toddlers) lack in ugly, they more than make up for in primitive: greedy, selfish, lazy, gluttonous, immature, and impulsive. And that's how it's supposed be; it's how we're designed. The whole point of parenting (if only) is to train a child to tame that primitive self that lives in all of us. Without the capacity to discipline one's pride, greed, gluttony, laziness, or selfishness, life is an uphill battle. Self-discipline begets employment, marriage, children, health, meaningful contribution to society, and peace of mind. Parenting is the ideal way, theoretically, to civilize uncouth youth. It only goes wrong if the parents aren't perfect.

And there's the rub.

Sell your books at sellbackyourBook.com!

Go to sellbackyourBook.com and get an instant price quote. We even pay the shipping - see what your old books are worth today!

Inspected By:margarita_qc

00060447359

0006044 **7359**

No parent is perfect, and some are more imperfect than others. All parents make mistakes; some parents make a lot of mistakes; a few parents make really terrible mistakes. Then the kids grow up and become parents themselves. Not a surefire recipe for success in any culture. One culture may have more or less alcoholism, more or less child abuse, or more or less divorce than another, but we all have it all. This in no way excuses any of our sins and failings, but it is imperative that we evaluate them in context.

I take it very seriously that real people are undergoing real suffering and that we all have an obligation to mitigate that suffering as much as possible. The only way to do that is to tell the truth and take a good hard look at ourselves in the process. The truth is that the finest cultures have terrible flaws and the basest cultures have noble aspects. Nothing is all good or all bad. Even the Taliban built some schools.

But let's get down to our own brass tacks, shall we?

Slavery, Jim Crow, and Segregation

It's time to revisit our friends the Greeks for just a minute. We're going to be going around the mulberry bush for a bit, but trust me, it will make sense in the end.

The wonderful, fabulous, stupefying Western civilization started by the Greeks didn't last. Not even for them. A few hundred years into it, the Greeks got themselves a couple of those yucky empires: Athens and Sparta. There went the independent city-states. War this, war that, conquest this, conquest that, the Peloponnesian War, conquest of Athens by Sparta, escape of Athens from Spartan rule, defeat of all Greeks by Philip of Macedon, and then—drumroll please—the assassination of Philip, which brought his son Alexander the Great to the throne. A the G was a military genius; by the end of his 13 year rule, the Macedonian Empire included Greece, Persia, and Egypt.

What goes up must come down, and after a little interlude with Hannibal, Antony, and Cleopatra, Rome took over the entire Hellenic world. After conquering Carthage and Greece, Roman soldiers advanced into Gaul, Spain, Persia, Palestine, Egypt, and, eventually, Britain. The Romans loved them some Greek art, architecture, and gods—Greco-Roman, anyone?—but not philosophy, innovation, or democracy. Those days were over.

The republic that ruled Rome initially was better than the tyrants who ruled Eastern empires but not by much. A small group of very wealthy landowners—men of course—called themselves the Senate and ran the whole show. They made themselves and their elitist friends *fabulously* wealthy with booty and slaves from military victories. Someone should have been there to whisper, "Be careful what you wish for" in their ear because that booty and those slaves were their downfall.

The unending supply of cheap slaves destroyed the population of independent farmers as their land was bought up (or taken) to form the Roman version of plantations—*latifundia*. Displaced farmers flooded Rome and, with no means of supporting themselves, became a politically unstable and perpetually hungry group of malcontents.

If you've never heard the term "bread and circuses," let me be the first. Bread and circuses are rumored to be the first known social services in history. (I don't know that for sure, but it sounds like it might be true.) To placate the displaced malcontents, every Roman city gave out bread, olive oil, and wine, and staged huge spectacles in arenas. Isn't it so true that you can always find someone worse off than yourself? The malcontents had to feel better, don't you think, as they watched lions tear Christians limb from limb?

Without independent farmers' sons to supply Rome with its

citizen-soldiers, it turned to a professional army, an army only too happy to back a tyrant holding out the promise of immediate rewards. A bit of nasty business with Julius Caesar ended with his assassination in 44 BC. For the next 14 years, the Roman Republic and the Roman Empire vied for top dog. In 31 BC Octavian as Caesar Augustus ascended the throne as the first emperor of Rome.

PLEASE ENJOY THIS BRIEF INTERMISSION

Rome rises, *really* rises, gets too big for one person to rule, is divided under four rulers—the tetrarch—and morphs into an East Roman Empire and a West Roman Empire. The East Roman Empire AKA the Byzantine Empire is not our concern; it lasted a whole lot longer than the West Roman Empire.

In the West, a lot of (kind of boring) military conquests happened. The Romans withdrew from Britain to fight barbarians in other parts of the empire. Britain was invaded by the Saxons, the Picts, and the Scots. The Huns pushed westward into Roman territory. Rome was sacked not once but twice; the Visigoths in AD 410 and the Vandals in AD 455.

WE NOW RETURN TO OUR REGULARLY SCHEDULED FALL OF ROME

Finally, finally, finally, and not a moment too soon, the West Roman Empire fell, and thank heaven it did because there would have been no modern Europe without its tumble. Yeah, yeah, everyone thinks Rome was so great, and parts of it were, but it was also huge, repressive, and stultifying. The best thing that ever happened to the West was the fall of Rome.

[It would be wrong of me to leave our discussion of the Roman Empire without sharing the wonderful imagery of the emperor Nero in the summer of 64 in his garden at night. He would cover Christians in wax, impale them on poles shoved up their rectums, and set them on fire—fully conscious—to give light to his yard.[21]]

As the empire broke apart, hundreds of independent, small scale political units took its place throughout Europe. The social experimentation and creative competition gave us:

- Towns and cities that were centers of trade and manufacturing. What disappeared were Roman cities that had been funded by the government and existed only for collecting taxes, administering local rule, and quartering troops.
- An industrious people who didn't eat if they didn't work. What disappeared was the idle class.
- Increased trade in practical things like iron tools and weapons, pottery, glassware, and woolens. What disappeared was the flow of luxury goods—exotic food, jewels, coins, precious metals, and cloth from foreign lands—*to* Rome, and the flow of tax collectors and soldiers back *from* Rome, i.e., not trade at all but traffic.
- Regular access to animal protein by all members of society.[22] What disappeared were the extreme social stratifications that had influenced dietary intake in Rome.

Yes, arts and literature took a hit initially. People who are focused on feeding their families don't have time to paint. They don't have time to write either. They work their tails off. There were always people working their tails off who didn't have time to paint or write, but during the empire, they were heavily taxed to support the idle class in Rome. It was the leisure class who had the luxury of time to paint, write, and sculpt. When the empire fell, painters and writers and sculptors had to work to eat, too.

An Italian scholar in the 1300s by the name of Petrarch, i.e., someone with Latin-ish skin in the game, looked askance at the decline of Latin literature after the fall of Rome and dubbed the era "dark." Enlightenment thinkers were only too happy to pick up on the derogatory term because, clearly *Dah*-ling, their own "enlightenment" was absent from the period.

Meanwhile.

In AD 771, a guy named Charlemagne found himself in charge of a whole heckuva lot of what today we call France and Germany. This Charlemagne guy was on a mission to unify all the Germanic peoples under one kingdom so he started conquering everybody he could left and right: the Lombards, the Avars, the Saxons, and others. The Saxons held out longer than anyone, some thirty years, but Charlemagne was ruthless (who knew?). He ordered more than 4,000 of them slaughtered at the Massacre of Verden in 782. And then, because conquering them wasn't enough, he insisted they all convert to Christianity or be killed. Persuasive. They did it.

Charlemagne was kind of a fanatic—they called him a "zealous" defender of Christianity—and Pope Leo III thought it would be a good idea to leverage that whole thing. Pope Leo crowned him Holy Roman Emperor on Christmas Day in 800. (Was it called Christmas Day back then? I don't think so.) Charlemagne laid the ideological foundation for a politically and religiously unified Europe. Because of Charlemagne, European civilization was born.

Back to Slavery, Jim Crow, and Segregation

That was an awfully long way around the mulberry bush, I know, to come back to slavery, Jim Crow, and segregation. But if I've said it once, I've said it a thousand times: context is king. If I had jumped directly from the highly evolved, intellectual and philosophical Greek civilization to Uncle Tom's Cabin, I would have misled you.

The early Athenians gave birth to something unique because they were the right people at the right time under the right circumstances to do it. They were the first to realize that human life wasn't cheap, but that doesn't mean they knew how valuable it was. Rome did nothing to advance that ball; one could even argue they made life cheaper. When our Founders took the best of Western civilization to make a country, true understanding of the value of human life was still in its infancy.

Now we're at Uncle Tom's Cabin.

Slavery

Okay, it's time to put on our Big Girl Truth Panties (shout out to Iyanla Vanzant). Are you ready? All cultures had slaves. (By "all," I mean at least 99.9999999 percent of them.) Long before Europe was a speck in her daddy's eye, Egypt enslaved Hebrews; Greece enslaved people acquired in wars or through trade; Rome enslaved people captured in war and even their own citizens; and Africans enslaved each other. This last category is controversial, as you can imagine, so it bears scrutiny.

(BTW, none of the foregoing excuses anything Europeans did, and it was Europeans who took slavery up a few reprehensible notches. But we're all about context right now.)

Of course Africans enslaved each other; it's almost insulting to imply that they didn't.[23] Before the first Europeans on Africa's West coast, Africa had powerful empires and at least one sophisticated urban settlement (Mali). Ancient Ghana flourished in gold trade from at least the 8th century.[24] Most enslaved Africans were captured in battles or kidnapped, and some were sold into slavery for punishment or repayment of a debt, but slavery in Africa was more like indentured servitude. For example, the powerful Ashanti nation allowed their slaves to marry, own property, and own their own slaves. Slaves were not inherited, and their children weren't born as slaves. After a certain number of years of servitude, the Ashanti freed them.

Africans also sold each other to European slavers for a handsome profit. The powerful kingdom of Benin profited immensely from the slave trade, first with the Portuguese, who arrived in 1441,[25] and later the Dutch and the British.[26] African leaders encouraged competition between the Dutch and the British to drive up the price. Slave traders exchanged humans for iron, alcohol, guns, gunpowder, mirrors, knives, cloth, beads, and other items brought by boat from Europe.

There are plenty of online sources claiming that Africans enslaving Africans is a myth. Or that it was simply how they survived colonization. What it was really was a reflection of how cheaply life was viewed at that time. African slavery existed long before Europeans landed on the West coast of Africa and continued long afterward. Africans treated their own slaves more humanely, but they had no illusion about the brutal slavery awaiting those they sold to the Europeans.[27]

It's all about context. We're tracking the value of human life down through history. Slavery was universal and unquestioned, both before and after the Golden Age in Athens when it first occurred to anyone that human life is precious—a miracle that idea if you think about it. The concept seems to have taken a hit during the Roman Empire with Nero and his fully-conscious Christian candles, and the willingness of Rome to enslave its own citizens, but it survived. Enlightenment thinkers picked up on the concept and really made it shine. By the time America was America, it was on fire. If you were white.

And that is the darkest part of the darkest part of our underbelly. We have to own it.

American Slavery

Slavery in America was unspeakably brutal. I can't possibly do rightful injustice to it in words on a page, but I'll do my best. Slaves had no dignity, no power, no independence, and no rights. They were pieces of property (chattel) from the time they were born to the time they died, which was of old age for the lucky ones. They had no right to their children, who were born as the property of whoever owned them and could be sold at any time for any reason. Women had no right to control their own bodies and gave birth to half-white children after being raped by slave masters or overseers. Their lives were one long chain of degradation, inhumanity, and pain, lived in humiliating fashion for all to see.

Just take a minute. Let that sink in. If you have no empathy for the anger many blacks feel today, you need to get some. How can any thinking, feeling human being whose ancestors endured slavery be neutral? How can any thinking, feeling human being aware of the horrors of slavery be neutral? Decency requires anger in all of us. And it requires sorrow and disgust. It also requires knowledge of context.

Blacks were the epitome of powerless in this country for 245 years. But this country was formed from the best of Western civilization, and the hallmark of Western civilization is reason and progress. We have a fundamental belief (and evidence) in the ability to reason our way forward to a better future. Along the way from slavery to Jim Crow (in some ways worse than slavery[28]) to segregation to the Civil

Rights Movement to President Barack Obama, a lot of the people doing a lot of the progressive reasoning were white.[29]

There were white people who savaged blacks and white people who gave their lives for black freedom and equality. The only difference between the two is the degree to which American values—freedom, equality, justice, democracy—took hold in those individuals. A superficial understanding of those values, or their absence altogether, is the source of other ills we've caused and cause and faced and face. An abbreviated list includes:

- Forced resettlement of Indian tribes onto reservations.
- Robber barons and other instances of rapacious capitalism.
- Child labor and child abuse.
- Interment of Japanese Americans during World War II.
- Homophobia.
- Sexism.
- Opioid and other drug epidemics.
- Entitlement.
- Ingratitude.
- Indifference.

We have work to do. Work that will never end because we live in a country where reason and progress are the only constants. Pick any of the list above or one I haven't mentioned and consider how reason and progress can make a difference. That is what sets Western civilization apart and, as Western civilization's crowning jewel, it is what sets America apart.

Key Points
- Like all cultures, our American brand of Western culture has an ugly side.

- We can't solve problems if we don't identify them correctly, and we can't identify them correctly if we don't look at them honestly.
- Slavery, Jim Crow, and segregation are a heinous blight on our country that we can never erase.
- Likewise our treatment of American Indians.
- Slavery existed everywhere in the world, but the Western world was the first to eliminate it; Africans both enslaved and sold each other to the British and the Dutch.
- The fall of Rome was a good thing because it unleashed independent and creative entities that eventually became Europe.
- Western culture is never satisfied because reason and progress are always showing us where we need to improve.
- America is the crowning jewel of Western civilization.

America Is the Worst Country
There Is—Except for all the Others

There's no sugarcoating it; we've got issues. In fact, based on the last chapter, it looks like we're pretty rotten. And in many ways we are. But now it's time to look at ourselves in comparison with other countries in the world. If it has never occurred to you that we might actually be better than other countries in the world, you might be suffering from utopianism. That's a disorder where you believe unrealistically that utopia is possible, and you are and will be in continuous distress until it happens. (Inside baseball tip: You have to *want* to be in distress all the time to make it happen.)

Utopia is like the missing tile syndrome only it's a mindset not a reflex. When we look at a group of tiles, if one of them is missing, our eye goes automatically to the hole. When we look at our country, if we automatically think of the negative, that is what we will see and all that we will see. To see the positive as well, we have to interrupt the negative mindset by considering context. Some among us would actually prefer to focus on the negative, but we'll cover that in "Nobody Wins at the Victim Olympics."

It's important as we consider the positive that we not slip into utopianism's nemesis: complacency. Complacency is a disorder where we are so comfortable and unchallenged in life that we forget other people aren't so lucky. When we take up space and resources on the planet, we're obligated to make effort on others' behalf. Sorry. That's just how it is. Electronics, *The Walking Dead*, and no bad hair days are great, but they do nothing for anyone else. You have the right to live a totally self-centered life, but please refrain from complaining about the state of the world if you do.

Let's begin our tour, shall we?

The Easy Wins

Brazil – Rich natural resources naturally (no pun intended unless it's funny and then, yes, I totally intended it) attract those who would exploit them for gain. In 2015, 185 environmental activists were murdered worldwide; 50 of them in Brazil.[30]

Japan – During WWII, hundreds of thousands of Korean "comfort women" were forced to be sex slaves for Japanese troops, reportedly servicing 30 to 40 soldiers a day.[31] [Note: This isn't happening today, we hope, but it's intense enough to make it onto the list.]

India – The 3,000 year old Hindu caste system deems the lowest caste—Dalits—less than human and impure. Originally outlawed in India's constitution in 1955, the practice of "untouchability" is so entrenched that additional strictures were implemented in 1976 and again in 1989. Still there are instances where members of higher castes will not touch anything that has come into physical contact with the "untouchables." Dalits *are forced* to work in the dirtiest, most menial jobs where they suffer discrimination and human rights abuses.[32]

Russia – People dying of cancer can't get morphine. At least 27 cancer patients in several Russian regions committed suicide in 2015, reportedly due to untreated, cancer-related pain. (If you know anyone with cancer, or have suffered it yourself, you know the pain is beyond excruciating. We treat our dogs better.)[33]

Somalia – Ninety-eight percent of women and girls aged 15 to 49 years have at least one living daughter who has undergone Female Genital Mutilation (FGM).[34] Tradition and social norms require that girls undergo FGM to make them socially accepted and marriageable, and to uphold the status and honor of the entire family.

China – Fundamental human rights—freedom of expression, association, assembly, and religion—are systematically curtailed. Chinese citizens are subject to arbitrary detention, enforced disappearance, politicized prosecutions, and torture. The government censors politically unacceptable information on the Internet with a "Great Firewall." Official approval is given to only five recognized religions, and the government controls religious personnel appointments.[35]

Iran – Iran Human Rights (IHR) reports at least 530 people were executed in the Islamic Republic of Iran in 2016, including five juveniles. IHR is aware of nine women who were executed, but only two were announced by official sources. Public hangings in front of children are commonplace.[36] The last stoning reported by IHR was in 2009,[37] but there are individuals in Iranian jails today who have received that sentence and are at risk of it being carried out. It is still legal.

Cuba – People are detained to prevent them from participating in peaceful marches or meetings to discuss politics. They may be held for hours or days, without the ability to communicate with anyone, and they are often beaten.[38]

Yemen – Houthis and other armed groups recruit, train, and deploy children in manning check-points or carrying arms. In the 10 weeks between 3/26/15 and 6/16/15, 279 children were killed and 402 were injured.[39] The government signed a UN action plan in 2014 to end the use of child soldiers but, chaotic as it is, has been incapable of implementing it. An estimated 3,600 schools are closed, affecting 1.8 million children.[40]

Saudi Arabia – Non-Muslim public places of worship are prohibited, and the courts prosecute and imprison people for dissent, apostasy, and blasphemy. A 2014 decree makes the promotion of atheism an act of terrorism and is used to target human rights defenders, especially those who advocate women's participation in society. The US State Department and the United States Commission on International Religious Freedom both deem Saudi Arabia a "country of particular concern."[41]

Obviously, you don't need a gun to your head to know you'd rather live in America than any of the countries above.

The Not-so-Easy-but-Still Wins

The competition is stiffer when we talk about countries in Scandinavia or Western Europe, but I can still make the case.

A word about the evaluation process before we go on.

You might think that the only fair way to compare countries is with hard data from a reliable source. You would be wrong. I hate to break it to you, but you can make statistics say virtually anything you want. There's a reason for the expression "Lies, damn lies, and statistics." For example, let's see who the World Health Organization (WHO) thinks has really great healthcare.

WHO collects data on a set of specific health measures in 191 member countries, including life expectancy at birth; skilled health professional density; new HIV infections; and prevalence of over-weight children.[42] Until about 20 years ago, WHO published an overall rank for every country in addition to a rank of countries on each individual item.

In their last report with an overall country rank, WHO used estimates from 1997 to determine the ten countries with the best healthcare systems: [43]

1. France
2. Italy
3. San Marino
4. Andorra
5. Malta
6. Singapore
7. Spain
8. Oman
9. Austria
10. Japan

The United States ranked 37th on the list, behind Columbia and Costa Rica, and only two spots ahead of Cuba. WHO rates our healthcare system only marginally better than Cuba. Hopefully, this makes no sense to you. It should make no sense because it isn't true. You don't need a WHO report to know that.

Real world example: Your mother has a rare heart condition. Do you want the surgeon who operates on her to be in:

A. Havana
B. Los Angles
C. Neither (you've never been fond of the old lady)

How in the world (I could make another pun/not pun joke here, but it's probably getting old) does the World Health Organization rank us only two spots ahead of Cuba? Easy. They stacked the deck with the questions they asked.

All WHO had to do was ask about universal health coverage, inequalities in coverage, and out-of-pocket payments for healthcare services. You see, to them, universal access to crappy healthcare, as in Cuba, is awesome, but imperfect access to world renown healthcare is a travesty. I'm afraid I don't find the WHO's rating of healthcare systems to be of much informational value, unless the information you're seeking is of an ideological bent.

Freedom of the Press

Let's say you want to know how our freedom of the press compares to that of the rest of the world. If you want to compare freedom of the press around the world, you would first have to decide whose data to trust (always the riskiest part of any research effort). If you're a super-perfectionist Type A personality, you would probably want to use two sources to verify that the information you're examining is reliable. Reporters Without Borders and Freedom House are very different types of organizations that each claim to be the definitive source on global freedom of the press.

(It's only fair to warn you that you're about to read just about the tightest, most fact-checked set of paragraphs you've ever encountered, and it is accordingly chock full of data. Only the truly wonky need proceed. Everyone else can skip down to "Mano a Mano AKA Bring It.")

In 1985, four journalists established Reporters Without Borders in Montpelier, France as an advocacy group for journalists and bloggers in danger. (The office is currently located in Paris.) They lend bulletproof vests and helmets, give training to journalists in physical and digital security, and provide insurance and an emergency hotline to journalists traveling to war zones or covering elections in dangerous regions.

Since 2002, they have published an annual World Press Freedom Index that is "quoted by media throughout the world and is used by diplomats and international entities such as the United Nations and the World Bank." The report evaluates pluralism, independence of the media, quality of legislative framework, and safety of journalists in each country. Data is collected by means of a questionnaire sent to journalists, media lawyers, researchers and other media specialists. This qualitative analysis is combined with quantitative data on abuses and acts of violence against journalists during the period evaluated.[44]

Freedom House was established in New York City in 1941 as a bipartisan watchdog in response to the threat of Nazism; later they defended against communism. Since 1980, they have published an annual Freedom of the Press Report that is "the most comprehensive data set available on global media freedom and serves as a key resource for policymakers, international institutions, journalists, activists, and scholars worldwide." Using a methodology devised by leading social scientists, data is collected on a series of media freedoms: legal environment for the media, political pressures that influence reporting, and economic factors that affect access to news and information.[45]

Each of these two credible organizations collects and analyzes relevant data to produce a report; each touts their own report to be *the* report you can trust. How surprised will you be if they produce different stats? You haven't been paying attention if the discrepancy between them raises even one eyebrow.

In 2016, Reporters Without Borders found the least repressive countries to be:

1. Norway
2. Sweden
3. Finland
4. Denmark
5. Netherlands
6. Costa Rica
7. Switzerland
8. Jamaica
9. Belgium
10. Iceland

The United States is 43 on the Reporters Without Borders list, behind the Czech Republic, Latvia, Chile, Belize, and Burkina Faso.

In 2016, Freedom House found the least repressive countries to be:

1. Norway
2. Sweden
3. Finland
4. Netherlands
5. Belgium
6. Denmark
7. Switzerland
8. Iceland

9. Costa Rica
10. Ireland

The United States is 17 on the Freedom House list, tied with the Czech Republic and before Latvia, Chile, Belize, and Burkina Faso.

How can this be? Could it be the way the deck is stacked, I mean, the questions are structured?

As one example, Reporters Without Borders asks in their questionnaire:

- *How well do media reflect the population's language diversity?*[46]

Well, it depends. How do "journalists, media lawyers, researchers and other media specialists" view "language diversity" in America? Are we talking English and Spanish? If so, are the plethora of Hispanic media outlets good enough? Or are we talking other minority languages as well?

We have to provide election materials in Chinese, Tagalog, Japanese, Korean, and Vietnamese; why not media outlets? In December 2016, the Census Bureau updated to 263 the number of jurisdictions that must provide foreign language assistance per the Voting Rights Act.[47] If five percent or 10,000 of voting age citizens in a jurisdiction are of a given language minority, and do not speak or understand English well enough to participate in the electoral process, they must be provided election materials in their own language.

Within the 263 covered jurisdictions, 5,118,191 citizens of voting age require assistance in a language other than Spanish. What is the minimum number of people that trigger a media outlet in their language? Is it considered "repression" if they don't get it?

An even better example comes from the Freedom House questionnaire:

- *Do high-level government leaders contribute to a hostile environment for the press, for example by engaging in repeated animosity toward or negative verbal rhetoric against the media?* [48]

Well, it depends. From one side of the aisle, the answer is a resounding "Yes!" President Trump, Steve Bannon, and Sean Spicer have all engaged in negative verbal rhetoric against the media. (Hostile tweets should be its own category on the questionnaire.) From the other side of the aisle, the answer is a resounding "No! He's only defending himself against the toxic media!" Even if both sides agree that there's a hostile environment between high-level government leaders and the press, do they agree whose fault it is? If it is the fault of President Trump, that weighs against freedom of the press in this country. But what if it's the media? Can they repress themselves by being hostile toward the president? Do they seem repressed?

By now you should be convinced that statistics are not your friends. But I can hear some of you Googling away, trying to prove me wrong because both studies put Sweden at the top. Sweden Sweden Sweden. (Recall the Brady Bunch episode where Jan is peeved that "Marcia Marcia Marcia" is getting all the attention.) All right then, let's go in for a closer look at Sweden.

Sweden, glorious Sweden, with its utopian utopia has a press that's the freest of the free...maybe. If you read the fine print, you'll see that Sweden has a Press Subsidies Council—*Presstödsnämnden*—whose job it is to "safeguar[d] the diversity of the daily newspaper market."[49] How does one safeguard diversity? With money, of course. It's the job of the subsidies council to dole out money so that "diverse" newspapers can remain financially viable.

Is it just my capitalism talking or is "subsidy" a rose of repression by another name? Freedom implies "free," as in flying without a net.

When the government gets involved in deciding who is worthy of viability, and props up selectees with cash, it at the very least represses market forces. But, wait, don't the extremely high rates of taxation in a welfare state repress a few market forces themselves? (see Curve, Laffer[50]). Maybe Sweden isn't as free as utopians thought.

Mano a Mano AKA Bring It

To get that America is the best country there is, you have to believe your lying eyes. The first thing your lying eyes should tell you is that we can't be compared to any other country because there is no other country like America. There never has been, and there never will be.

Pick a metric, any metric.

Healthcare. Good choice. How many times have you heard someone say the healthcare system is better in Sweden? (That blasted Sweden.) Sweden can tout its success all it wants, but addressing the healthcare needs of a homogenous nation (at least until recently) of 10,000,000 is a snap compared to the complexities we face. It's like bragging you got an "A" in math when it's the only class you're taking while someone else got only a "B" but is taking four other classes and working full time.

Real world example: Your family is a hot mess (don't feel bad—a lot of us are), and you're considering a move to Sweden. Why? Because Sweden. Duh. Because you're a super-perfectionist, Type A personality, you do your homework on how well Sweden can meet your family's healthcare needs.

You – take Vyvanse for depression and are mighty relieved to have found the only medication that works for you. You tried Zoloft, but it made you nauseous. Effexor killed the...should we call it "happy ending?" in the bedroom, and Prozac made you feel like a zombie. All the other medications stopped working after a while, which your doctor has told you is very common.

You search "Vyvanse" in Sweden's handy-dandy database (those Scandinavian countries are so efficient) but are horrified to find that it's not available in Sweden.[51] Sweden's healthcare system allows only generic medications, and Vyvanse is under patent until 2023.

(Your overly helpful and know-it-all brother-in-law begins to lecture you on the merits of non-profit medical systems, but you don't have time to put him in his capitalism-deprived place.)

Your wife – is starting early menopause at the age of 42. What with all the hoopla of considering a move to Sweden, she has put off going to the doctor about her mood swings and hot flashes. She'll have to start treatment in *Sverige* (Sweden).

You learn that Hormone Replacement Therapy (HRT) is used to treat early onset menopause in Sweden, and you're stoked. You've read your share of medical studies. You know that HRT, while controversial, may give post-menopausal women some protection against cardiovascular disease.[52] All the women in your wife's family seem to die from heart disease, and none of them have had breast cancer, so your wife's doctor has strongly advised her to take HRT despite the potential risks.

Sadly, you were distracted by an unfortunate incident with your Rottweiler and missed the most relevant medical study. It appears that HRT may be seriously underutilized in Swedish women with early onset menopause, both because it is prescribed in extremely low numbers and because most women who take it stop in less than a year. Apparently women with early onset menopause are recommended to take HRT until the average age of menopause (51-52), or they are at increased risk of cardiovascular disease, neurological disease, osteoporosis, psychiatric illness and even death.[53] Who knew? You'll wish you did.

Your daughter – has the BRCA1 cancer gene.[54] You were so upset when you found out, but control freak that you are, you're now almost smug with how much research you've done. Thanks to the National Cancer Institute, you know that 39 percent of women who inherit the BRCA1 mutation will develop ovarian cancer by age 70. Because the National Institutes of Health (NIH) maintains meticulous statistics, you've been able to research the mortality rate for ovarian cancer as well. Between the years 2010-2014, the incidence of mortality in white women with ovarian cancer was 7.7 per 100,000.[55]

You just know Sweden's mortality rate is going to be better. Because Sweden. You excitedly search through Sweden's national statistics database on cancer.[56] It's *so* high tech. You can slice and dice the stats any way you want. You set the parameters for "ovarian cancer," "all of Sweden," "0-85+ years," and "2010-2014." Now all you need is to run the report for mortality rates, and you can compare apples to apples. Wait...what? Mortality rates aren't available in the database? Only number of new cases?

You're confused, because you could have sworn the American Cancer Institute says mortality rates are the best way to measure cancer stats. After all, with the way technology gets better all the time, more cancers may be detected sooner, and that would obviously make the number of new cases each year go up. That would be fine if you could swear the rise in new cases was only because of the improved technology catching more cancers sooner. But you can't know for sure, so those statistics aren't really that helpful.

Hmm. You wonder how Sweden knows whether their cancer treatments are effective. Oh well.

Your son – has extreme ADHD. Now this is the one that you care most about. You adore your son, but he's a cross between Tigger and a fire hose. You don't even like to remember the dark days before he was properly medicated. The trial on Concerta was especially bad. When he found out that some other kids were playing without him, he kicked all their bikes over. No meds at all was better than Concerta, but barely. Thank heaven your doc knew your son's system would respond best to drugs in the amphetamine family. That was a close one!

(Your overly helpful, know-it-all brother-in-law has a new lecture for you on the sin of medicating kids with ADHD. "Think of the side effects," he says. You're still super busy, but you can't stop yourself from sharing a bit of perspective you got from the psychiatrist. "There are all kinds of side effects to ADHD, treated or not. Medication has side effects, but so does always getting in trouble and annoying your peers.")

You go to the handy-dandy Swedish government database and search Adderall. Nope. Dexedrin? Nope. Vyvanse? You don't even need to search that one. Not to fear. In 2012, Consumer Reports published a study on the best ADHD medications.[57] You'll just check that. Ooops. Of the seven families of ADHD meds, Sweden only offers four. Maybe they're the best four. Ooops. That can't be right. Sweden allows no amphetamines, dextroamphetamines, or lisdexamphetamines. In fact, Sweden seems to have a real thing against them. Of the top 40 medications listed by Consumer Reports, Sweden offers only seven.

This is not good. If you move to Sweden, you'll have to start the search for an effective Depression med all over again. You're not sure how good your daughter's chances will be if she gets cancer. You don't know why, but you have a bad feeling about your wife. And now, you realize Junior will be bouncing off the walls without the family of drugs his system responds to best? What is it with these Swedes?

Maybe you should look into Norway.

(Note: I have nothing against Sweden. In fact, my family had a Swedish exchange student when I was growing up whom I adore. We're still very close, and Sweden is the only European country I've taken my children to visit. My Swedish sister is an MD (free, free, free education), and the Swedish people couldn't have been lovelier when we there. But I'm like Jan Brady with "Marcia, Marcia, Marcia." I just get so tired of being compared to Sweden, Sweden, Sweden.)

The Real Win

Do you really want to know what makes us better—yes, better, I said it—than any other country? It's our lightning in a bottle meets perfect storm meets the American brand of Western culture. (Note: If you are *still* complaining that we stink as a country, snore. I already agreed with you, let it go. We're going to focus on the positive now.)

We inherited our Western culture through our cultural pro- genitor Britain. The first Americans were British before they were American, and they bequeathed us the fruit of the Enlightenment, the Renaissance, the Industrial Revolution, and the Magna Carta. What's the Magna Carta, you ask? Only the first document in recorded history that made the king subject to law like everyone else. Our Founders were thinking of the Magna Carta's guaranteed rights and liberties when they wrote our Bill of Rights.

Another uniquely Western right came to us from Rome through Britain—the concept of private property owned *by the individual*—without which there is no prosperity in the truest sense of the word. We in America took it to a whole new level. We enjoy so much prosperity in this country that even our poorest citizens have color televisions, indoor plumbing, and cell phones. That is a level of prosperity enjoyed in the rest of the world by only the middle class.

When Western culture arrived here, it landed on a vast continent bounded by nothing but the Pacific Ocean on one side and the Atlantic Ocean on the other. When American culture spread from the mountains to the prairies to the oceans white with foam, it was spread by people with courage and the spirit of adventure. They risked leaving the comforts of home and family for a new world. Not just from the Old World to America but from settled America to the frontier. When we say we're a nation of immigrants, we're saying we're a nation of courageous, adventurous people. What do you get when you mix courageous, adventurous people with freedom and individualism in a land of limitless possibilities? You get America.

The Real America

Back in the day, every high school student knew Alexis de Tocqueville and his 19th century reality show about America AKA *Democracy in America*. (Back then, reality shows were in the form of books written after personal observation and interaction.) A de T was a Frenchman of aristocratic lineage who found himself on the wrong side of the tracks, so to speak, when the monarchy changed hands in 1830. He was no dummy and got himself a little project out of town until the heat died down. Tocqueville asked for and received official permission to study prison reforms in America.

Once here, Tocqueville found himself a whole lot more curious about our political and social life than our prisons. He spent nine months talking to us, observing us, and marveling, frankly, at what he saw. Lucky for us, he wrote it all down. It's like finding your grandmother's diary and seeing who she really was before she was just the mother of one of your parents.

What impressed him most of all were our attempts at equality, which, by today's standards, don't look like equality at all. But *in context*, our early attempts at equality made us *radically different* from the rest of the world. Tocqueville was amazed to see men shaking hands with each other like equals. He had never seen it before, coming from a world where the nobility did not touch the commoner, and the higher the noble, the lower the bow or curtsy of the commoner. It was so bizarre to see such equality in social relations that he worried no one would believe him back home.

He observed a deep respect for the law in our people, which he attributed to our ultimate power to change any laws we didn't like. In America, unlike anywhere else, the people gave the law to the government and not the other way around.

Tocqueville found us to be fools for voluntary associations. The Greeks had already invented play, but we Americans apparently invented hanging out with a purpose: political parties, debating clubs, women's missionary and charitable societies, temperance societies, musical societies, and associations to found Sunday schools and plant trees. Europe had nothing like it. In Europe, either the government did it or it didn't get done.

He also noted potential downsides to our love affair with equality and identified the American solution for each.

- Tyranny of the majority happens when those in power exercise that power in cruel and oppressive ways. *The Supreme Court can rule laws unconstitutional.*
- Excessive focus on the individual makes us turn in on ourselves and neglect our civic duties. *The American jury system forces us to think about other people and educates us in the use of our freedom.*
- Materialism occurs when people think they ought to have as much wealth as anyone else. *Religion focuses us beyond the material world.*

He observed other problems that had no solution, then or now. We tended to get a little full of ourselves. He found our politicians lacking in knowledge and integrity. The drive for equality worked against freedom of thought because to express an opinion contrary to the majority was an act of inequality, i.e., setting oneself above the majority. (Today we call it political correctness.) You may be amused to know that we've always gone a little cray-cray during presidential elections.

> *Long before the appointed moment arrives, the election becomes the greatest and so to speak sole business preoccupying minds.... For his part, the president is absorbed by the care of defending himself. He no longer governs in the interest of the state, but in that of his reelection...As the election approaches, intrigues become more active, agitation more lively and more widespread. Citizens divide into several camps.... The entire nation falls into a feverish state; the election is then the daily text of public papers, the subject of particular conversations,*

the goal of all reasoning, the object of all thoughts, the sole interest of the present.[58]

Tocqueville saved his harshest criticism for slavery and our steady extermination of the Indian tribes. He witnessed one of our darkest moments in Memphis, Tennessee when the last of the Choctaw Nation was led onto a boat at the end of their Trail of Tears.

This whole spectacle had an air of ruin and destruction; it spoke of final farewells and of no turning back. One felt heartsick watching it. The Indians were calm, but somber and taciturn.[59]

And he witnessed one of our shining moments in Albany, New York during an Independence Day celebration:

It was as though an electric current moved through the hearts of everyone there. It was in no way a theatrical performance. In this reading of the promises of independence that have been kept so well, in this turning of an entire nation toward the memories of its birth, in this union of the present generation with one that is no longer and with which, for a moment, it shared all these generous feelings, there was something profoundly felt and truly great.[60]

That's us. The worst and the best. We're the worst country there is. Except for all the others.

Key Points

- It isn't helpful to look at America in isolation; only in context of what other countries have been able to accomplish do we see our true success.

- You can make statistics come out any way you want; think critically when you hear something as ludicrous as our healthcare rates 37th in the world and only two slots above Cuba.

- Sweden is great, but it isn't America.
- When we say we're a nation of immigrants, we're saying we're a nation of courageous, adventurous people and their descendants.
- Alexis de Tocqueville was so shocked at the egalitarian culture of early America that he was afraid nobody back in France would believe him.
- He was disgusted by our treatment of American Indians, and we should be, too.

People Are Equal;
Cultures Are Not

P eople are equal. Why does this even need to be said? A baby born in India in 1930, a baby born in Britain in 1820, and a baby born in Botswana today all have equal worth, equal value. The differences between them as individuals are superficial: hair color, eye color, skin color, blood type, etc. The differences between them as members of different cultures, however, are profound. People are equal. Cultures are not.

An easy way to see this is to look at two different colonial powers in the New World: Spain and Britain.

Spanish Colonies in Hispaniola

Columbus has gotten a bad rap lately, and while I have no time for his defense at the moment, I submit that he has been woefully maligned. Can we agree that he was the one who proved you could sail across the Atlantic from Europe and back? (He did so you better.) The recorded history of the Western Hemisphere begins with him, which is no small thing either.

Columbus sailed the ocean blue in 1492 for Queen Isabella and King Ferdinand of Spain, the "Catholic Monarchs." Spain wasn't Columbus's first choice of patron, but beggars can't be choosers. For their part, the royal couple didn't really think he'd be successful but knew that if he were, he might bring back untold riches. So Isabella and Ferdinand purchased the 15th century version of a lottery ticket. If Columbus didn't make it, no big loss. But if he *did* make it, Ferdinand could replenish the royal coffers, and Isabella could impose her beloved Roman Catholicism throughout the New World. She and Ferdinand had already done a bang-up job of imposing it throughout Spain with the help of a little something called the Spanish Inquisition. Isabella loved Christianity so much that she Christian-loved the Moors and the Jews right on out of Spain, i.e., expelled them. It's a thin line between love and hate.

Columbus didn't find a direct water route from Western Europe to Asia, but he found something almost as good: gold in Latin America. Spain was the first country to have a permanent European settlement in the Western Hemisphere, in Hispaniola (present day Dominican Republic). This is where the Columbus-maligning opens its ugly maw, but like I said, no time. One of the first orders Columbus gave his men was to "range about the country and make the Indians acquainted with the power of the Spaniards, that they might learn to fear and obey them."[61] We all know what happened next, but the relevant part is *how* it happened.

Columbus sent gold nuggets back to Isabella, and pious, orthodox Isabella sent Spaniards over to convert the Indians to Christianity. In hot pursuit of gold, Spaniards quickly overran and overtook Hispaniola, Puerto Rico, Jamaica, and Cuba. They founded cities in Panama, Mexico, Chile, Argentina, Brazil, and Peru. In their greedy path, entire tribes were made extinct, most notably the Aztecs in Mexico and the Incas in Peru. The ones who survived were forced into Christianity and then into servitude in mines or on plantations. At its peak, Spain had dominion over all of Central America and almost all of South America.

Draining the New World of its wealth by means of a huge, imperial system, Spain exploited minerals, land, and people to finance the expansion of its global empire. At its peak, Spain was the largest empire in the world, the largest European empire since ancient Rome. It was said first about Spain that the sun never set on its empire. (At the risk of insulting your intelligence, that means that as the earth traveled around the sun every 24 hours, there was not a moment where the sun's rays were not illuminating something belonging to Spain). And what do empires do? That's right. They crush. From all the way over in Spain, the monarchy ruled the Spanish colonies in the Americas with a tight empire fist.

The king controlled all economic activity. The king was chosen by God and had supreme power over everything and everyone. How handy that the Roman Catholic Church was able to clarify that to disobey the king was not only to endanger your life but to *condemn your mortal soul.* Individuals in the Spanish Empire, or should I say subject to the Spanish Empire, had no rights at all, not even to life itself.

When Latin American colonies began one by one to gain their independence from Spain, they—surprise, surprise—replaced imperial rulers with local despots: Santa Anna, Somoza, Pinochet, Chavez, Castro, etc. It's all they knew. It's all they know.

British Colonies in America

It was said later of the British Empire that the sun never set upon it, and the British Empire did its share of crushing, for sure.

It seems like this would be a good place to acknowledge how cruelly we treated American Indians both before we won our independence from Britain and after. For most of us, American Indians are "out of sight, out of mind," which is almost worse than the way they got there. If you dare, read *The New Trail of Tears: How Washington Is Destroying American Indians* by Naomi Schaefer Riley, but be forewarned: you will be angry enough to do something about it when you're done.

The British Empire was heavily influenced by the Germanic tribes that poured into the Western half of the Roman Empire. There is some debate as to where the Germanic tribes originated, perhaps Scandinavia, perhaps Gdansk in modern Poland, but wherever they came from, they brought a fiercely independent spirit and a practice of electing their leaders. The Magna Carta is the heritage of that independence and shared government power. The British Empire, in sharp contrast to the heavy-handed Spanish Empire, governed its colonies in America by a charter of liberties.

This part of the Magna Carta should ring a bell:

No freeman is to be taken or imprisoned or disseised of his free tenement or of his liberties or free customs, or outlawed or exiled or in any way ruined, nor will we go against such a man or send against him save by lawful judgement of his peers or by the law of the land. To no-one will we sell or deny of delay right or justice.[62]

We call it the Fourth Amendment:

The right of the people to be secure in their persons, houses, papers, and effects, against unreasonable searches and seizures, shall not be violated, and no Warrants shall issue, but upon probable cause, supported by Oath or affirmation, and particularly describing the place to be searched, and the persons or things to be seized.

The English Bill of Rights in 1689[63] included free elections, freedom of speech, limits on taxation, freedom from cruel and unusual punishments, and the separation of powers.

We also call ours the Bill of Rights.

The culture of Britain/England dignified and promoted the worth of the individual, and the American colonies inherited this culture. Our Founding Fathers were imbued with individualism as they pledged to each other their lives, their fortunes, and their sacred honor. Influenced by the Magna Carta, Platonic ideals, Roman law, and Enlightenment thinking, the Founders established an American culture of limited government, individual rights, private property, and free market economics.

The Americas Today

I could detail differences between our culture today and that of our neighbor to the south, but aren't you a little tired of my crackerjack research? (I'm a little tired of preparing it.) Plus, you need to take over the reins of your intellectual journey for yourself at some point. I will simply pick one example from each continent to illustrate what the different cultures have produced.

In Venezuela, the people have no food. They are eating flamingoes, and stray dogs and cats they find in the streets.[64]

In America, we have landed on the moon. We have already retired the space shuttle program we used to launch satellites, fix the Hubble Space Telescope, and transport astronauts to the International Space Station. Why? Because now we're working on a program to send astronauts to Mars.

There is not one iota of difference in intellect or capabilities between a baby born in Venezuela and a baby born in North Dakota. They're equal as equal can be. When each is 50 and a product of their respective cultures, will the result show that those cultures are equal or not equal?

By the by, I think I've hit on an absolutely marvelous analogy for America as the epitome of Western culture. Are you ready? Go with me here. Consider the space shuttle. At T-minus 6 seconds, the solid rocket boosters are ignited, the bolts that secure the shuttle to the ground are explosively released, and at T-minus 0 seconds, the orbiter rockets into the sky. It is the rocket boosters that provide the additional thrust the space shuttle needs to escape the earth's gravitational pull.

At around T-plus 2 minutes, having fulfilled their purpose, the solid rocket boosters separate from the orbiter, descend on parachutes, and land in the Atlantic Ocean. (In case anyone wants to know, they are recovered by ships, returned to land, and refurbished for reuse.)

Once the space shuttle is free of the earth's gravitational pull, it needs to be put in orbit. To accomplish this, two orbital maneuvering system (OMS) engines are fired twice for 316 seconds.[65]

Fun fact #1: "T" used to stand for "time," but in our high tech world, it now stands for "test."

Once in orbit, the ship would stay in perfect orbit if space were completely empty. But it's not. It's empty but for miniscule specks of floating matter. Over time the orbit degrades because of millions of tiny collisions with floating matter. NASA scientists estimate that the space shuttle can stay in orbit for about a month before the cumulative force of the collisions slows it enough that it falls out of orbit.

Fun fact #2: Sometimes NASA scientists will "dip" a satellite into the atmosphere of a planet on purpose so that drag will slow it. This is called "aerobraking."

What does the space shuttle have to do with America as the epitome of Western civilization?

The early Greeks ignited Western civilization. Their intellect and passion are the rocket boosters that allowed revolutionary ideas about the worth of individuals to break free of what had always been: the view of humanity as expendable resources for their empires. The Enlightenment is the first thrusting sequence. The European intellectual movement of the 17th and 18th centuries fine-tuned individualism and reason. The United States Constitution and the Bill of Rights are the second thrusting sequence. Our founding documents codify and exhort us to the purest ideals of individualism and reason. With them, we achieved perfect orbit: the epitome of Western civilization.

Today what's going on with our Western civilization epitome? Our American brand of Western culture is degrading from the millions of not so tiny collisions with those who would disdain it. Vilify it even. At this point, we have experienced so much drag that we've "culture-braked" it. But if NASA scientists can put a ship back in orbit using an orbital maneuvering system, we can put America's Western culture back in play with the Constitution and the Bill of Rights. It's never too late.

Watch *Apollo 13* with Tom Hanks for inspiration. The entire story is a thing of awe, but there is one scene that exemplifies American Western culture in a chill bumps kind of way. This isn't Hollywood—it really happened.[66]

Scene
Interior – Mission Control – Day/Night/Who Knows
There's a problem with the carbon dioxide levels on the lunar module (LEM) because it is equipped for only two guys for a day and a half. Without a moon landing, there are three guys in the LEM, and it's going to be a lot longer than a day and a half. As carbon dioxide levels increase beyond a certain threshold, the astronauts will begin to experience impaired judgment, blackouts, and the beginnings of brain asphyxia. There are carbon dioxide scrubbers in the command module, but they take square cartridges, and the ones on the LEM are round.
Flight Director Gene Kranz, Mission Control: "Well, I suggest you gentleman invent a way to put a square peg in a round hole...rapidly."
A NASA employee dumps out onto a table a large box full of the same equipment available to the astronauts on Apollo 13.
NASA Employee: "Okay, people, listen up. The people upstairs have handed us this one, and we gotta come through. We gotta find a way to make this (*holds up a square cartridge*) fit into the hole for this (*holds up a round scrubber*) using noth-

ing but that (*nods toward the equipment dumped out on the table*)."

And, of course they do. Because they (and we) have a fundamental belief in our ability to reason our way through problems. They (and we) are astonishingly innovative. And for some awesome reason, we have a lot of natural optimism. It took equal parts optimism, confidence, and innovativeness to bring the Apollo 13 astronauts home safely.

Because in America, failure is not an option.

Key Points

- Of *course* people are equal. Duh.
- People are shaped in large part by their cultural environment, and we can compare cultures by comparing the learned behavior of people living in them.
- The Spanish Empire colonized Latin America in the old school way of controlling everything; a peasantry and rife corruption were the natural outgrowth, both of which last until today.
- The British were influenced heavily by the Magna Carta when they colonized North America; equal rights and freedoms were the natural outgrowth, which last until today.
- The process of a Space Shuttle launch is akin to Western civilization's launch of America.
- *Apollo 13* is a great movie.

We Can Be Forgiven for Our Sins

I bet you think this chapter is going to be about Christianity, but you're wrong. I could, if I wanted, wax poetic for quite some time on how Christianity is only possible in the West, and how Christianity embodies the West's essential characteristics: a rational God and the ability to progress in our knowledge of him and his creation.

I could dispel the oft-repeated (and apparently believed) canard that science and religion are incompatible. I could name early scientist after early scientist whose belief in God shaped his pursuit of knowledge: Galileo, Bacon, Kepler, Pascal, Newton, Faraday, Mendel, Kelvin. I could note the University of Paris, "the first true university in the West," whose distinction was the teaching of theology. I could also note that the University of Oxford in England was modeled after the University of Paris.[67] I could show how the influence of Western thought—humanism and the Renaissance—challenged the unquestioned infallibility of the Roman Catholic Church AKA The Holy Roman *Empire*.[68]

The Renaissance began in Italy and remained a largely secular phenomenon there, but as it expanded to Northern Europe (German-speaking countries, France, and England), it became the chief means of attempts to reform the Catholic Church. In Northern Europe, most humanists were devout Catholics. The notion of critical thinking and the rejection of authority unless it arose from reliable evidence affected one Martin Luther very much. The Protestant Reformation, an entirely religious undertaking, was inspired by humanist ideals. (Understanding of contemporary complex issues would benefit from incorporating opposing points of view, don't you think?)

However. This chapter is not about Christianity. It is about a principle that resonates with Christianity but is not dependent on it, namely forgiveness.

Forgiveness is the releasing of someone from obligation with no remaining acrimony. (That's my own definition, but I think it's pretty good.) Defining forgiveness this way makes it relevant to excusing debts, letting go of hurt, and recognizing that people are capable of learning. It's the latter category we're interested in here.

Remember what I said about complex issues benefitting from opposing points of view? Here's your chance to let it happen`. In the Christian world, forgiveness cannot be understood apart from repentance. Understanding of the principle of repentance furthers our understanding of the principle of forgiveness. My favorite definition of repentance is "a change of mind, i.e., a fresh view about God, about oneself, and about the world."[69] Is that not exactly what we want when we look at historical evil? The Germans are one of the best examples of this. Angela Merkel received a standing ovation in the Knesset when she said Germans are filled with shame for the Holocaust.[70]

Merkel's apology was not the first from Germany and will likely not be the last. Does anyone doubt the remorse the German people feel over their country's role in the mass murder of six million Jews? Can they be forgiven? Not Hitler and Goebbels and Göring, but contemporary Germans who weren't even alive during WWII? They can do nothing to change the past. The best they can do is acknowledge the pain their forebears caused. The best we can hope for is that they've learned in remorse (for those living at the time) and shame (for everyone) how to prevent it from happening again.

It's important to note that we cannot (should not) be forgiven *in* our sins if we are still committing them. How sincere is remorse if the behavior doesn't stop? How can there be healing if there isn't true remorse? How can we move forward if there's no healing? It's also important to note that none of the above is automatic. There are people in this world for whom nothing is enough, and maybe they're justified in some cases. I can't judge. I do know that a willingness to move forward comes more easily to those whose pain is fully and completely acknowledged.

American Indians

I am not in a position to offer forgiveness for our treatment of American Indians, but from where I sit, their pain has not been fully and completely acknowledged. Nor have we stopped sinning against them. Unless you have some personal reason for knowledge about the state of Indian affairs, you are likely completely ignorant as to how bad it still and truly is. Like I said in the last chapter, "out of sight, out of mind" might be worse than how they got there. When you hear the term "1 percent" you probably think of Mark Zuckerberg or Oprah, but there's another 1 percent: the bottom 1 percent of poverty that live on Indian reservations.

In 1831, Chief Justice John Marshall ruled that Indians:

> *...are in a state of pupilage. Their relations to the United*

States resemble that of a ward to his guardian. They look to our Government for protection, rely upon its kindness and its power, appeal to it for relief to their wants, and address the President as their Great Father.[71]

This is known as the Indian Trust Responsibility and remains in effect today.[72] In short, the federal government in its infinite wisdom deems Indians incapable of owning or managing their own land. All of their assets are managed by bureaucrats *on their behalf*, and every important decision they make requires approval from Uncle Sam. Usually with a boatload of regulations.

When Indians do not own their land:

- They cannot use the land as collateral to get loans, e.g., for starting a business.
- They cannot easily develop natural resources like coal, oil, and natural gas. To acquire a permit for energy development on Indian lands, private companies are required to go through four federal agencies and 49 steps. To acquire the same permit off Indian lands requires only four steps.[73]
- They are legislated out of the free market economy. Alcoholism, corruption, and school dropout rates are the symptoms, not the problem.

There is no prosperity without property rights. There is no excuse for depriving Indians of their property rights. As long as we deprive them of their property rights, IMHO, we cannot be forgiven.

Black Americans

Is there a more loaded term than "racist" or "racism" in our society today? Once the shadow of that word has darkened your door, whether accurate or not, you're finished. Just ask Paula Deen. In 2012, Paula

Deen was accused by a former employee of racially insensitive talk and employment practices that were unfair to black workers. Deen was asked during a deposition if she had ever used the N word. "Yes, of course," she answered.[74]

Among the fallout from her admission, the Food Network did not renew her contract, Walmart and Target dropped her product line, and she lost several lucrative endorsements. Not that context is allowed to matter, but further along in the deposition, Deen stated, "But that's just not a word that we use as time has gone on. Things have changed since the '60s in the south."

Paula Deen was born in 1947 in Atlanta, Georgia. When President Johnson signed the Civil Rights Act of 1964, she was 17. Quick! Cast your mind about for a 17 year old you know today. Is he or she the arbiter of intelligence, good taste, and maturity? "Not so fast," you may say. "Deen admitted to using the N word even after 1964." And I would say, "Quick! Cast your mind about for someone you know who has decided to stop a behavior—swearing, smoking, drinking, overeating, etc." I think you can see where this is going.

But for the sake of argument, let's assume Paula Deen was an avowed racist until well into her 40s. The lawsuit against her was filed when she was approximately 65. When the case was settled a year later, Deen's accuser made a very interesting statement:[75]

*During a very difficult period in my life the Deen family gave me hope and the opportunity to work to build a brighter future for my family and me. I assumed that all of my complaints about the workplace environment were getting to Paula Deen, but I learned during this matter that this was not the case. The Paula Deen I have known for **more than eight years** is a woman of compassion and kindness and will never tolerate discrimination or racism of any kind toward anyone. [emphasis added]*

Either Paula Deen had not been racist for many years; or she did a good job pretending not to be racist for many years; or she had excellent legal counsel that negotiated the conciliatory statement from her accuser. I like to give people the benefit of the doubt, so I'm going to go with a combination of all three.

The moral of the story is that people can learn. People can change. Are you the same person you were 15 years ago? For your sake (and your loved ones'), I hope not. And if you're up on some high horse that *you* have never used the N word, good for you. I'm sitting on the same horse, but I'm not foolish enough to lift myself up for it. We are social animals, and we socialize the way we are taught. I wouldn't hold it against you if you had said the N word before you realized how demeaning it is, as long as now that you've realized it, you've banished the word from your vocabulary and call people out for using it in your presence. And if you didn't use the N word, you did something else that makes you cringe looking back. None of our poop smells like roses. And if you say yours does, I don't believe you.

Maya Angelou said (and I'm paraphrasing), "You did what you knew. When you knew better, you did better." We want learning to count for something. We want to know and to teach our children that effort and sincerity make the world a better place. We want to know that our value is not in our perfection but in our contribution. Take a good hard look, and you'll see that some of the most powerful forces for good are powerful precisely because they used to be bad.

Is the transformation of Saul on the road to Tarsus not the best story ever? Saul persecuted Christians. He killed them, took parents away from their children, did the worst of the worst of the worst to them. Probably overflowing with self-righteousness the whole time. After he learned and changed, who did he become? Paul, the greatest evangelist ever. Should God have kicked Paul to the curb because he had already sinned as Saul? Think about what the world would have lost. Paul was as effective as he was at least in part because the gospel transformed his own life, and he was able to teach others with the power of that knowledge.

What about former gang bangers who leave that life and work with law enforcement to help other youth escape? Or former jihadists who overcome that poisonous worldview and make it their mission to protect the rest of us?[76] It may not happen often, but it does happen, and don't you think former baddies are the most effective at thwarting current baddies?

Our value isn't in our perfection but in our contribution.

I don't like people who have never fallen or stumbled. Their virtue is lifeless and it isn't of much value. Life hasn't revealed its beauty to them.—Boris Pasternak

The Founding Fathers

A word about solipsism. Solipsism is the theory that only the self exists or can be proved to exist. The 21st century version of solipsism is an extreme preoccupation with and indulgence of one's feelings, desires, etc. AKA egoistic self-absorption.

Solipsism leads (some of) us to believe we are all that has ever been or ever will be. We can't conceive of a past where things we take for granted weren't known by everyone. We believe our Founders understood slavery exactly the way we do and owned slaves anyway. And we can't conceive of a future where people take for granted things we've never known. (I would give an example, but I can't cite what I've never known.) Solipsism is illogical. Aristotle would be very disappointed.

The West is about progress. You can't have progress without a starting point, and the starting point is never as good as where progress takes you. It isn't a defect that we used to be more racist as a society; it's a tribute to our progress that we aren't as racist now. And for anyone out there suffering from delusions of utopia, give it up. We will never be devoid of racism. Not as long as humans walk the earth. We have eradicated all *legal* forms of racism. The subtle, insidious forms are still there, more visible to some than to others, but denying the progress we've made does nothing to further the progress we still need to make.

We're the West. We will never be satisfied with where we are because we have a fundamental belief in our ability to reason our way forward to a better future. That's what we do. That's how we got *here*. We can be forgiven for being *there*.

Key Points
- It isn't necessary to invoke Christianity to talk about the failings and redemption of Western culture.
- We need to keep ourselves humble with a sense of shame about how we've treated certain groups in the past.
- Feeling guilt over slavery is counterproductive because it implies responsibility, and we can do nothing to change the past.
- We can condemn people to live in their ignorance or hurtfulness forever, but there's no point in denying that people are capable of learning and growing.
- Judging people of the past by today's knowledge is just as unfair as us being judged by Americans 200 years from now for our knowledge today.
- If we don't allow ourselves to move on, we'll never move on. Is it worth it?

Nobody Wins at
the Victim Olympics

Who wouldn't want to win a gold medal at the Olympics? With a medal come admiration, lucrative endorsements, and sometimes even a parade. Competition at the Victim Olympics is just as intense, but there are no winners. The only way to "win" at the Victim Olympics is to prove you've suffered more discrimination than anyone else. The only sport at the Victim Olympics is jockeying for most harmed victim group status. No medal is conferred, but the most victimized group gets to wear their status as a badge of honor called "moral authority." Moral authority is the all-access pass to winning debates and popularity contests, and landing coveted, well-paid jobs in academia.[77]

Gone are the simpler days of yore when blacks claimed victimization by whites, women claimed victimization by men, and gays claimed victimization by straights. Today we have racism, sexism, classism, ableism, transphobia, xenophobia, and "belief-based bigotry." Today it's all about the *degree* of victimization because each victim group can be subdivided into more specialized victim groups: gender, race, social class, ethnicity, nationality, sexual orientation, religion, age, mental disability, physical disability, mental illness, and physical illness.

It's a perverse, reverse pecking order where the more categories of oppression someone can lay claim to, the more weight their experiences, voices, and ideas carry. White women have the advantage of race but are penalized by gender; they have the least moral authority at the table. Black women are penalized by gender and race, so they have more moral authority. Latina lesbians are penalized by ethnicity, gender, and sexual orientation. A disabled, black, Muslim, transgender woman on welfare could write her own ticket in the moral authority universe.

This is not your mother's victimhood. This is 21st century victimhood. It's called "intersectionality" and is just a fancy way of saying, "there's always more victimhood where that came from."

Intersectionality

Intersectionality is "the interconnected nature of social categorizations such as race, class, and gender as they apply to a given individual or group, regarded as creating overlapping and interdependent systems of discrimination or disadvantage."

Overlapping and interdependent systems of discrimination or disadvantage. Mmmm. How do I get me some of that? And what does that look like in real life, say, at the Women's March on January 21, 2017? It looks (and smells) like hygiene-challenged (I'm talkin' to you, AJ) chaos. Black women were mad that white women had too prominent a role. Transgender women felt excluded by genital-based women. "Woke" white women were annoyed with their "unwoke" white sisters who wouldn't atone for their whiteness and shut up. Abortion activists refused to allow a pro-life feminist group to sponsor the event.

How is a single one of these groups a winner? Not to mention the waste of time, intellect, and energy they spent on conflicts with each other when they could have been self-righteously thinking about blowing up—Madonna-style—the White House. If we on the sanity side of the equation want to eliminate intersectionality, we should just encourage it; it is fundamentally self-destructive.

Affirmative Action

Of course it makes sense for the larger society to affirmatively address disadvantages it caused by unfair treatment of minorities historically, and to a certain extent we do. We have a federally-mandated affirmative action[78] program for government contractors. Colleges and universities may consider race as *one factor* in a narrowly-tailored admissions process. The majority of need-based scholarships go to minorities.[79] And many top companies voluntarily commit resources to increase minority hiring, promotion, and retention, e.g., diversity task forces and advisory committees.[80] None of these alone qualify minorities for the Victim Olympics. That takes a little something extra.

To compete in the Victim Olympics, minorities must *assign 100 percent of the blame* to the larger society for their failure to achieve, succeed, or prosper in the present day. They must promote or reinforce racist interpretations of, well, just about everything. If their answer is "racism" no matter the question, they're on the team.

I reiterate my commitment to alleviating real suffering by telling the truth about it and then doing something about it. Discrimination is wrong in every circumstance, and I will be the first to call out anyone who practices it. Honestly, I will. When I was five, I stood up to an entire playground of kids who were bullying one little boy. I *hate* bullying, and I *hate* arbitrary unfairness. But as angry as I feel toward bullies, I feel at least as angry toward people who deliberately fan racial flames. Why? It doesn't hurt me all that much in the end, but it's wildly unfair to spoon feed a diet of "racism, racism, everywhere racism" to young people.

What young people lack in maturity and wisdom, they make up for in idealism. Life is bruising, and idealism sputters out sooner or later, but it shoots us skyward while it's on fire. Race-baiters who literally *train* young people to see racism everywhere they look are doing them no favors. It's a lot harder to succeed in school, on the job, or in life when you identify first and foremost as a victim.

Note: The following sections refer to Regents of University of California v. Bakke, 438 U.S. 265 (1978).

Case in point. In *Regents of the University of California v. Bakke,* the Supreme Court ruled that it was unlawful for UC Davis Medical School to set aside 16 places in a class of 100 for minorities.[81] In 2015, a Yale law professor—a woman named Linda Greenhouse[82]— wrote of that decision: [83]

> *Justice Powell **was bluntly dismissive** of any claim that the exclusion of African-Americans from access to medical school in the past justified special consideration in the present. "The remedying of the effects of 'societal discrimination,' he warned, was "an amorphous concept of injury that may be ageless in its reach into the past."* [emphasis added]

Put yourself in the shoes of an African-American who wants to go to medical school today, or the shoes of an African-American whose parent or grandparent was not able to go to medical school because of racial discrimination. Doesn't reading Justice Powell's decision make your blood boil? It does mine. What makes my blood boil more is actually reading *Bakke*. It seems Greenhouse omitted a few details.

1. The court upheld the California Supreme Court's decision that UC Davis's special admissions program was unlawful because it operated as a *racial quota*.

2. The court *reversed* the California Supreme Court's decision that race could *not* be considered as a factor in admissions.

Held: The judgment below is affirmed insofar as it orders respondent's admission to Davis and invalidates petitioner's special admissions program, but is reversed insofar as it prohibits petitioner from taking race into account as a factor in its future admissions decisions.

Writing for the majority, Justice Powell said:

(If your eyes start to glaze over, just read the bolded parts.)

If petitioner's purpose is to assure within its student body some specified percentage of a particular group merely because of its race or ethnic origin, such a preferential purpose must be rejected not as insubstantial, but as facially invalid. **Preferring members of any one group for no reason other than race or ethnic origin is discrimination for its own sake. This the Constitution forbids.** *E.g., Loving v. Virginia, supra at 388 U. S. 11; McLaughlin v. Florida, supra at 379 U. S+. 198; Brown v. Board of Education, 347 U. S. 483 (1954).*

The State certainly has a legitimate and substantial interest in ameliorating, or eliminating where feasible, the disabling effects of identified discrimination. *The line of school desegregation cases, commencing with Brown, attests to the importance of this state goal and the commitment of the judiciary to affirm all lawful means toward its attainment. In the school cases, the States were required by court order to redress the wrongs worked by specific instances of racial discrimination.*

That goal was far more focused than the remedying of the effects of "societal discrimination," an amorphous concept of injury that may be ageless in its reach into the past.

We have never approved a classification that aids persons perceived as members of relatively victimized groups at the expense of other innocent individuals in the absence of judicial, legislative, or administrative findings of constitutional or statutory violations. See, e.g., Teamsters v. United States, 431 U. S. 324, 431 U. S. 367-376 (1977); United Jewish Organizations, 430 U.S. at 430 U. S. 155-156; South Carolina v. Katzenbach, 383 U. S. 301, 383 U. S. 308 (1966)... Without such findings of constitutional or statutory violations, [Footnote 44] it cannot be said that the government has any greater interest in helping one individual than in refraining from harming another. Thus, the government has no compelling justification for inflicting such harm.

*Petitioner does not purport to have made, and is in no position to make, such findings. Its broad mission is education, not the formulation of any legislative policy or the adjudication of particular claims of illegality...*Lacking this capability, petitioner has not carried its burden of justification on this issue.

Hence, the purpose of helping certain groups whom the faculty of the Davis Medical School perceived as victims of "societal discrimination" does not justify a classification that imposes disadvantages upon persons like respondent, who bear no responsibility for whatever harm the beneficiaries of the special admissions program are thought to have suffered. To hold otherwise would be to convert a remedy heretofore reserved for violations of legal rights into a privilege *that all institutions throughout the Nation could grant at their pleasure to whatever groups are perceived as victims of societal discrimination. That is a step we have never approved. Cf. Pasadena Cty Board of Education v. Spangler, 427 U. S. 424 (1976).* [emphasis added]

I'm not an attorney, but I pretend to be one in my mind sometimes. What I get from Powell's statement is:

- Admission based on race *alone* is unconstitutional, no matter which race it is.

- Because there has been historical discrimination against blacks, it is lawful to consider race as *one factor* in the admissions process.

- The special admissions program at issue was unlawful because UC Davis did not have the authority or capacity to prove that its racial classification was responsive to identified discrimination.

- UC Davis may continue to consider race as a factor in future admissions decisions.

What exactly is that "bluntly dismissive" of? Throughout the rest of the opinion, Powell evinces clearly that he takes historical discrimination very seriously.

*Green v. County School Board, 391 U. S. 430 (1968), gave explicit recognition to **the fact that the habit of discrimination and the cultural tradition of race prejudice cultivated by centuries of legal slavery and segregation** were not immediately dissipated when [the court], announced the constitutional principle that equal educational opportunity and participation in all aspects of American life could not be denied on the basis of race. Rather, **massive official and private resistance prevented, and to a lesser extent still prevents,*** *attainment of equal opportunity in education at all levels and in the professions. The generation of minority students applying to Davis Medical School since it opened in 1968 ...clearly have been victims of this discrimination.* Judicial decrees recognizing discrimination in public education in California testify to the fact of widespread discrimination suffered by California-born minority applicants; [Footnote 2/53] many minority group members living in California, moreover, were born and reared in school districts in Southern States segregated by law. [Footnote 2/54] Since separation of schoolchildren by race "generates a feeling of inferiority as to their status in the community that may affect their hearts and minds in a way unlikely ever to be undone," Brown I, supra at 347 U. S. 494, **the conclusion is inescapable that applicants to medical school must be few indeed who** endured the effects of de jure segregation, the resistance to Brown I, or the equally debilitating pervasive private discrimination fostered by our long history of official discrimination, cf. Reitman v. Mulkey, 387 U. S. 369 (1967), and yet **come to the starting line with an education equal to whites.** [Footnote 2/55] [emphasis added]

How does it serve anyone for a professor at Yale Law School to represent the court as insensitive to minorities? If it serves any white people, those people are losers and need to "get served."[84] It definitely does *not* serve minorities in the way it reinforces to them that they are surrounded by racism, even in the highest places; that they are victims and powerless to do anything about it. Most reasonable minorities would probably be satisfied with the consideration of race in admissions policies as long as it was done constitutionally, which is exactly what the court ruled. But they'll never get that chance because Greenhouse and her ilk are spoon feeding them a diet of "racism, racism, everywhere racism." So their blood continues to boil.

What's worse is that Greenhouse was writing in response to an op-ed written by someone whose blood was already boiling: Jedidah C. Isler, a black woman and National Science Foundation astronomy and astrophysics postdoctoral fellow at Vanderbilt University.[85] After oral arguments in *Fisher v. University of Texas*, Isler found herself "reeling from a psychological blow."[86]

Abigail Fisher, a white female, was not admitted to the University of Texas at Austin. She sued on the basis that their race-conscious admission policy was a violation of the Equal Protection Clause of the Fourteenth Amendment. During oral arguments, Chief Justice John Roberts asked what perspective a minority student would bring to a physics class, and Isler went *off*.[87] Roberts is questioning (as my pretend attorney self sees it) what difference it makes to e=mc² how much pigment someone has in their skin. Isler takes it as a throw-down that black students have to "justify their presence" when whites do not.

Black students' responsibility in the classroom is not to serve as 'seasoning' to the academic soup. They do not function primarily to enrich the learning experience of white students. Black students come to the physics classroom for the same reason white students do; they love physics and want to know more. Do we require that white students justify their presence in the classroom? Do we need them to bring something other than their interest?

Actually, we do. We require that everyone bring something other than interest, and that's knowledge, or at least aptitude. We also recognize that knowledge is not a level playing field. As so eloquently expressed by Justice Powell in *Bakke*, our long history of official discrimination makes it impossible for all but a few black students to come to a college physics class with an education equal to whites. It says *nothing* about their intelligence or justification for being there. How else do we overcome historical discrimination unless we specifically address the *basis* of that discrimination? It's not an insult to select blacks who have an interest in physics *and* demonstrate a keen, albeit undeveloped, intelligence for them. It doesn't make them "seasoning."

But why would such an obviously brilliant woman be so hung up on diversity? Maybe she reads Greenhouse's columns. In Greenhouse's response to Isler's op-ed, she wrote:

> *Here's the problem, as Chief Justice Roberts well knows: under the court's precedents, diversity isn't just one rationale for creating or maintaining a racially integrated student body. It is the only rationale. Ever since the Bakke cases nearly four decades ago, no other reason for affirmative action has passed constitutional muster in the view of the Supreme Court's majority: not equalizing opportunity, not redressing past wrongs....or opening previously closed doors. Only "diversity."*

Is that how you read the *Bakke* decision above? Me and my pretend attorney self thought it said race was an appropriate consideration exactly *because* of unequal opportunity, past wrongs, and previously closed doors. (If you take nothing else away from this book, know that unless you've seen it, heard it, or read it for yourself, it might not be anything like what you think it is.)

Isler is on the Victim Olympics team, and Greenhouse is her coach. They reinforce each other's "racism, racism, everywhere racism" because they reinforce each other's ideas about racism. At a certain point, it just becomes an echo chamber.

Ironically, the court decided in favor of the University of Texas, i.e., they are not violating a white student's constitutional right to equal protection by considering a black student's race as part of the overall decision. What does Isler want? That the court find *against* UT? That UT not be allowed to consider race in its admissions? How do you think that will work out for black students who are both exceptionally bright and exceptionally disadvantaged?

The Power of Guilt

Unfortunately, it isn't just the left that's not thinking clearly. Too many of us are feeling guilt over something we never did. How are you guilty for something you didn't do? If you're white, you're expected to feel guilty for slavery even if you had no ancestors in the country at that time, or your ancestors were too poor to own slaves, or were building the Mormon Temple in Salt Lake City, or all died in the Civil War trying to abolish slavery.

Let's say you *are* descended from the eight percent of American families who owned slaves in 1860.[88] Even if your ancestors owned slaves, slavery is not like the Catholic "original sin" that comes into the world as a mark on each new baby Catholic.

Women could not own land, inherit property, or vote for a very long time. Is every male born with a mark of toxic masculinity? Scratch that. Bad example. Here's a better one. Margaret Sanger, the famous eugenicist (that's a killer of undesirable people, or, if you prefer, a preventer of breeding by undesirable people), started Planned Parenthood. Does every Planned Parenthood clinic mark its employees with the scourge of bigotry and hate? Absolutely not. It's those of us who oppose the legacy of a eugenicist who are marked with bigotry and hate.

Guilt is a powerful tool for tattooing social conservatives with the mark of the beast, i.e., their membership in any group that has ever thrived, for any amount of time, at any point in our history. Mighty tempting, I grant you. If your ancestors were in the white, male, European group, look out! Even your knowledge is suspect because it came via "masculine" styles of learning.

Did you know that objective truth is inherently discriminatory to women and minorities? That's right. A feminist scholar says it's masculine to expect an individual to learn knowledge that is "static and unchanging." [89] It "promotes a chilly climate that marginalizes women" when they're asked to "draw accurate conclusions from scientific data presented in different formats." What needs to happen, obviously, and sooner rather than later, is acceptance of "knowledge [that] is constructed by the student and dynamic, subject to change as it would in a more feminist view of knowledge." (All hell would break loose if a *man* questioned a woman's ability to "draw accurate conclusions from scientific data presented in different formats.")

The problem, you see, are discriminatory words like "actually" and "in fact" because they mislead the student that some information is "factual and beyond dispute." I wonder if feminists would make an exception for measurements of temperature. Are the effects of temperature on rubber factual and beyond dispute? Or are they constructed by the student and subject to change? In 1986, the Space Shuttle Challenger exploded 73 seconds after liftoff because cold temperatures caused two rubber O-rings to fail the morning of the launch. Would a feminist view of temperature have prevented the catastrophe?

Racism

Race always has been and always will be the most loaded dynamic in our society for obvious and not exaggerated reasons. And there are people who have a vested interest in perpetuating the guilt and even shame we feel about it. The first group is black Americans who feel aggrieved, discriminated against, and trapped in the legacy of slavery.

NOTHING TO APOLOGIZE FOR: THE TRUTH ABOUT WESTERN CIVILIZATION

The second group is white Americans who "[covet] responsibility for black problems—or at least the illusion of responsibility—because there [is] so much moral and political power in the idea of delivering blacks from their tragic past."[90] Both of these groups are kryptonite to any real progress in race relations.

There is a difference between guilt and shame and between individual and group assignation of guilt and shame. When we're talking about an individual, guilt is constructive—"I did something wrong. I feel guilty. I won't do it again." Shame is counterproductive—"There's something wrong with me. That's why I did what I did. I can't fix it. I might as well not even try." When we're talking about a group or a country, shame is constructive, like the shame Germans feel about the Holocaust. Group shame is a collective humbling, which restrains the destructive impulse that led to the shameful behavior in the first place. Group guilt is counterproductive because it assigns individual responsibility for something outside of the individual's control.

(If you're wondering where I got my doctorate in shame and guilt, it was at the School of Hard Knocks.)

Reparations

I hear the slavery reparations crowd revving their engines so allow me to make a point or two. It would require the granddaddy of all multiple regression formulas to apportion reparations. Variables would have to include:

- Whether a black American's ancestors were enslaved;
- Whether a white American's ancestors owned slaves;
- A formula that calculates:
  - the amount of increased wealth white Americans enjoyed due to slavery,
  - minus the amount of decreased wealth the whole country

suffered due to the burning of Atlanta and the 600,000
Civil War dead who couldn't provide for their families,

o   minus any monetary advantages currently enjoyed by su-
perstar black athletes in the NFL, NBA, or MLB; and

• A formula for determining who is white and who is black, and
how black someone is.

I suspect this last variable is nigh undeterminable. Beyond the
issue of mixed-race heritage, there is the issue of race as a "social
construct." Rachel Dolezal, a freckle-faced white girl of Scandinavian heritage, identifies as black. Does she stand in the "I owe
reparations" line or the "I get reparations" line?

What Would Oprah Do?

For the sake of argument, let's say a perfect and just system of reparations could be worked out. Theoretically. Just like the possibility that
an infinite number of monkeys banging away on an infinite number
of typewriters for an infinite amount of time could produce Hamlet
by accident. (A zoo in the UK put this thought experiment to the
test. It placed a PC in the cage of six crested macaques. In only 30
days, the monkeys had typed five pages of the letter "S" and broken
the keyboard.)

Wouldn't it be quicker just to go to the library and check out the
collected works of Shakespeare? And if black Americans want a bigger piece of the American economic pie, wouldn't it just be quicker
to go get it? Graduate high school, take advantage of the plethora of
scholarships for underprivileged youth, wait until married to have a
baby, and keep a gratitude journal. It would be awfully helpful if the
black community would work to eliminate the destructive thought
that being educated is akin to "acting white."

Don't shoot the messenger. Disdain for education in the black community is nothing new. Comedian Chris Rock, who I consider the Voltaire of our day, did a comedy bit in 2010 on how the black community receives one of their own coming home with a master's degree vs. coming home from prison. Coming home with a master's degree gets criticism, sarcasm, and judgment; coming home from prison gets respect and much love. The bit is so rife with F-bombs I can't bring myself to link it here, but should you want to watch it, you can go to YouTube and type in "Chris Rock – Master's Degree." The most instructive part of the 1:09 clip is the way the audience busts up laughing over it. Clearly, the truth of it struck a nerve.

If All Else Fails, Blame "White Privilege"

This is extremely flexible as victim status goes. We all know whites have been privileged over non-whites in many ways, and we have to acknowledge that. But the beauty of "white privilege" is that you don't actually have to be privileged to qualify for it.[91] If you're white, you're automatically included because "[a]ccess to privilege doesn't determine one's outcomes, but it is definitely an asset that makes it more likely that whatever talent, ability, and aspirations a person with privilege has will result in something positive for them."

"White privilege" is the AP Racism class. Deploring racism and its effects is just the beginning. Advanced study requires that we take responsibility for the privileges some of us have received as a result of it. The "best students" then use "white privilege" to address racism on an individual and institutional basis

On the White Privilege Conference website, they reassure the melanin-challenged that "It is not a conference designed to attack, degrade or beat up on white folks." Perhaps not, although the line is very thin. If there's a problem in the room, as they see it, it's whites who do not acknowledge and work through the negative implications of "Whiteness" and are not "committed to equity and social change." In other words, there are "good" whites and "bad" whites. "Bad" whites are totally okay that most of the people studied in history classes and textbooks are white. "Good" whites feel ashamed that most of the people in our country's history were—*shhhh*—white.

Certainly minorities contributed more to our history than they have received credit for, but it doesn't change the fact that 99.99999 percent of what we accomplished, and it is nothing to shake a stick at, was accomplished by white males. Sorry. That's just how it is. We don't study WWII by minimizing men's accomplishments to make women feel more included. How would we teach the liberation of Auschwitz, the beaches at Normandy, Dunkirk, or POW camps without elevating the bravery and sacrifice of the men who accomplished them?

Let's include more voices in our history as we learn about them, but we only dumb ourselves down by displacing history's heavy hitters to do so.

The Price of Entry to the Victim Olympics

Victimhood as identity is a poison pill. Any short-term gain in moral superiority or potential long-term gain in economic benefit comes at an exorbitant price. In order to identify as a victim, you have to:

- live in a state of perpetual grievance, i.e., go around with a chip on your shoulder;
- relinquish control of your destiny, i.e., live as though you have no control over your life;
- sacrifice your autonomy to social programs and policies by which society tries to redeem itself, i.e., forfeit pride in your

achievements and self-respect in your ability to overcome obstacles;

- submit to the paternalism of authorities who restrict your freedom and responsibilities (in your best interest, of course), i.e., tacitly agree to act like a child who needs a babysitter; and

- mentally cripple your children, i.e., train them to see the world as an ugly place full of people out to get them where they can never succeed because of The Man.

Picture this:

A family comes driving into town from somewhere down the road and finds a wizened old townie seated on a park bench.

"Howdy," calls out the father. "We're looking for a good place to put down some roots. What kind of people live in this town?"

"Well," responds the Townie, "what kind of people live in the town where you're from?"

The whole family breaks into broad smiles, and the mother says, "Oh, they're wonderful. So kind and always willing to help anyone in need."

"That's the kind of people you'll find here," says the townie.
*****

The next day a different family comes driving into town from somewhere else down the road and finds the same wizened old townie seated on a park bench.

"Howdy," calls out the father. "We're looking for a good place to put down some roots. What kind of people live in this town??"

"Well," responds the Townie, "what kind of people live in the town where you're from?"

The whole family scowls, and the mother says, "Oh, they're awful. They gossip and backbite and never want to help anyone."

"That's the kind of people you'll find here," says the townie.

Key Points

- Some degree of leveling the playing field is warranted, e.g., Affirmative Action in some cases.
- Reparations for slavery would require a mathematical model worthy of Will in *Good Will Hunting*.
- When we confer moral authority and power on victims, we create more victims.
- If everything and everyone is racist then nothing and no one is racist.
- If the answer is "racism" no matter the question, you're looking at a professional victim (or a very canny politician).
- Intersectionality is the victimhood that keeps on giving; give these folks enough time, and they'll eat each other.
- The organizations in society whose *raison d'être* is combatting racism have a vested interest in seeing racism continue.
- It is pandering to victimhood to eliminate the study of essential actors in our history in favor of non-essential actors who happen to be minorities.
- It is functional abuse to train young people to look for discrimination rather than teach them how to overcome it.
- Participating in the Victim Olympics is volunteering for your own helplessness and rage.

What Western Culture Isn't

Western culture is not code for white people rule the world. It isn't cultural appropriation, and it isn't 'white privilege' (notice the air quotes). Those are charges leveled against America's Western culture in order to eviscerate it. You have to remember that in leftist circles, Western culture is unforgivably synonymous with white people, and white people, you must have noticed, are Public Enemy #1. White European-ness is the modern day Bubonic Plague. Anything it touches is immediately poisoned, and the poison proliferates exponentially.

In excessive, virulent form, AKA white supremacy, white European-ness *is* poison. You'll get no argument from me there. White supremacists hate and feel entitled to dominate and kill non-whites, Jews, gays, and Muslims   because—in the white supremacist's mind—they are inferior and "threaten the purity of the white race" or some other such nonsense.

Speaking for all decent white people everywhere, I say unequivocally that white supremacist ideology is asinine, dangerous, and needs to be squashed like a bug. I'll be the first one to start the squashing, should I ever run into one. But it's unlikely I will. I'm far more likely to run into whites, non-whites, Jews, gays, and Muslims who think my white European-ness is dangerous and needs to be squashed like a bug. These people are everywhere, especially in the media and higher education. They are often the nicest of people, and I would know. I used to be one myself.

UC Berkeley is a Petrie dish for anti-Americanism. I attended from 1981 to 1985 and, when I arrived, all I knew about America was that we:

- lived in a part of the world discovered by Columbus;
- were once a British colony;
- were a beacon of religious freedom for the Pilgrims who landed at Plymouth Rock in 1620;
- fought for and won our independence from England;
- set up a tripartite government with a balance of power between the executive, judicial, and legislative branches;
- have freedom of speech, religion, assembly, and the press;
- wave a flag representing the original 13 colonies and all 50 states;
- sing a national anthem—"The Star Spangled Banner"—that expresses our patriotism, bravery, and gratitude for freedom;
- fought a civil war over slavery;
- fought in two world wars, were attacked by the Japanese at Pearl Harbor, and liberated concentration camps in Nazi Germany;
- endured a Great Depression (my dad never threw away a paper clip),
- practiced segregation and legal discrimination until the Civil Rights Act of 1964 was passed;
- put a man on the moon;
- went all hippie in the 60s; and

- rationed gas in the 70s under a sweater-wearing, peanut-farmer president by the name of Jimmy Carter.

In high school, I read standard classic works of Western Civilization: *The Odyssey, The Aeneid, The Prince, Lolita* (it was the 70s), *The Republic, Democracy in America, The Iliad, Oedipus Rex, Paradise Lost,* and *The Divine Comedy.*

When I arrived at Cal, my attitude toward America ranged from indifferent (because I was a self-centered teenager) to positive. How long do you think it took Berkeley to disabuse me of my American-evils illiteracy? Seems to me it was from the very first day. In short order, I learned that we were racist, sexist, imperialist, homophobic, rapaciously capitalistic, and disgustingly religious (read traditional morals).

I bought it all, hook, line, and sinker, the way any self-respecting, totally unprepared, middle class white kid would do. Stupid country. Stupid parents. Stupid white people. And don't get me started on Republicans and Christians. The dirtiest words in my vocabulary (and there were some mighty dirty words) were "Phyllis Schlafly." Every person I knew thought Ronald Reagan was the anti-Christ.

Hopefully, I have convinced you that I was all in for the radical progressive worldview. I was actually notorious for it in certain pagan circles. So deeply did those early grooves cut that I still wince when I hear certain words: Christian, Reagan, Republican, NRA, pro-life. I'm actually a tad embarrassed to admit I'm a Republican, although the more time goes by, the more they deserve it.

Then, in the midst of my progressive Berkeley utopia, something happened. Ronald Reagan was re-elected.

I had been out of the country in 1980 when he was elected the first time, living as an exchange student in France. The 1984 election was my first, and there was no question in my mind that Reagan was the most evil white, Christian, Republican ever to walk the face of the earth, although really, that was redundant. I can still see the map of the United States the night he won. Lonely Minnesota (Mondale's home state) was the only blue state on the whole map. Every other state was red. Red, red, red, red, red. A little light flickered in my mind, and I thought, *Hmm. I wonder if there are other ways to see the world besides the way Berkeley does?*

I immediately quashed the thought like any self-respecting progressive would do and went on with my life. I graduated, got a job, sowed a lot of promiscuous oats, did a Tarot reading every day for 10 years, got married outside at night under the full moon, got divorced, and moved back to San Diego where, horror of horrors, I met a loser Mormon on my job (shameless plug for *One of Everything*, chapter 12, available everywhere fine memoirs are sold).

Things really went downhill after that. I joined the Mormon Church, got married in the San Diego Temple, adopted three siblings from the County of San Diego when I was 42, my husband was 56, and they were 8, 5, and 1 (*One of Everything*, chapter 14), moved to Utah, and aged. Significantly (see three adopted siblings, above).

At the age of 54—yes, 54 and proud of it—I am in the catbird seat of a double agent. I speak progressive and conservative, pagan and Mormon, love of country and hate of country, career woman and stay-at-home mom, married and divorced, addicted and sober, California and Utah, and English and French. Ask me anything. Really. If I haven't seen it or done it, it probably doesn't exist.

Having been raised in a world that was drenched in what's good about Western culture, I'm in a fairly good position to say what it is. Having been turned against Western culture for a very long, very sincere, very impassioned time, I'm in a very good position to say what it isn't. It isn't white domination, white supremacy, "white privilege," or cultural appropriation. It isn't any of the things I was taught because I was taught them as the sum total of Western culture. I was made to understand that Western culture in America is bad, and the only good Americans are the ones who see it that way.

Leftist Americans are convinced—absolutely convinced without the shadow of a doubt—that they and they alone have the moral high ground. They hate and feel entitled to dominate and destroy Christians, Republicans, and whites with traditional values because—in the progressive's mind—we are inferior and threaten the purity of white liberal guilt, or some other such nonsense.

(Why does that sound familiar?)

Why Can't Lefties Kill America's Western Culture?

The problem with leftist attacks on Western culture is that you can't destroy a culture without destroying a people, and people tend to resist being destroyed. This should not come as a news flash to anyone, but most of us of every stripe are reasonable people. Reasonable people tend to acknowledge sins and make amends wherever possible. Reasonable people also reach a point where—if they're demonized long enough—they have nothing left to lose. The Civil Rights Movement is a perfect example. Black Americans weren't going to take it anymore and were prepared to die in their quest for equal treatment with whites.

What the left seems to miss today is that white, Western European culture has been demonized for so long in America that it is in survival mode. Some of us might even be starting to feel we have nothing left to lose.

We whities know our culture for what it is: good, bad, and ugly. We've admitted to a lot of the bad, and, speaking for reasonable white people everywhere, I say unequivocally that we have the integrity to continue doing so. We've atoned for a lot of the ugly, and, I think I speak for reasonable white people everywhere when I say, "Uncle." We don't deny doing reprehensible things, but please take the bitter backlash boot off our ugly at some point. What's the alternative? We are punished eternally for doing reprehensible things? That's one way to go, but where are the winners in that scenario? To forever cast our essential identities as either victims or victimizers is an unforgivable waste of intelligence, talent, energy, and hope for the world.

Increasingly, we want the good parts of Western culture acknowledged. Norman Rockwell paintings don't represent racism, homophobia, or religious bigotry because it wasn't there. It was there in the larger world but not in the world he was painting. The world that he painted existed alongside the ugly one, and some of what he painted shows the clueless oblivion of that insulated world, but a lot of what he painted captures its innocence, its happiness, and its hopefulness. That is the heritage of an awful lot of us, and just like other cultures want to honor their roots, so do those of us from white, European culture. The very same culture that embodied the concepts of reason and progress we used to abolish slavery; grant universal suffrage and civil rights; and invent the toaster, the car, the pacemaker, and the first workable prototype of the Internet.

Like it or not, white, Western European culture has been the dominant culture in America since its founding. No removal of monuments, flags, or historical information will change that. Western culture is not the apotheosis of human culture; it is just another step (a pretty fantastic one) along the way. America now reflects more diversity of cultures because Americans are more diverse.

That's a good thing. Nobody wants to go back to the 50s. We want to be in the 21st century with all that we've learned about ourselves and with rich appreciation for the contributions of a variety of cultures. Including white, Western European culture.

From my 54 year old catbird seat, I know that America is all of it: science, imperialism, progress, materialism, commercialism, slavery, reason, technology, innovation, homophobia, courage, racism, generosity, optimism, patriotism, kindness, integrity, corruption, aggression toward other countries, protection of other countries, capitalism, rapacious capitalism, religious idealism and religious bigotry. In other words, we're the worst country there is. Except for all the others.

> *Fun fact from the 1970s time capsule* – *When we rationed gas, it was by license plate. If your license plate ended in an odd number, you could gas up on odd-numbered days; even numbers could gas up on even-numbered days.*
>
> *Fun fact from the 1960s time capsule* – *It was very common to hear kids on the playground defend something they said or did with, "It's a free country."*
>
> *Poignant fact from the 1930s time capsule* – *When my mother was a little girl in Northwest Texas, there were drinking fountains for "white" and drinking fountains for "colored." She drank out of the colored fountain because she thought colored water would come out of it.*

Key Points

- Western culture is a lot of good things and bad things, but it isn't evil or irredeemable.
- It isn't the culture that ate other cultures or wants to.

- There is more than one way to see the world, and the more experience you have, the more accurate your view.
- People who think they derive moral authority from their politically correct views define anyone without their views as evil.
- The left has been trying to kill off Western culture for decades but hasn't succeeded because you can't kill off a people.
- If you push a people too hard, they push back.
- White, Western European culture is the backbone of this country. Deal with it.

What We Lose if We Lose Western Culture

Western culture is about reason, freedom, progress, and individualism. Which one are we willing to lose first? The sad thing is that they are all eroding and have been for some time.

Individualism

We are already a long way toward losing individualism. When was the last time you heard primacy given to individuals? All that matters anymore are groups, to which the individual is subordinated to the point of becoming a non-entity. Transgender bathrooms are a perfect example. How many transgender Americans are there? A UCLA report in 2016 puts the number at 1.4 million adults (shout out to Hawaii with the highest percentage of adults who identify as transgender at 0.8 percent).[92] The 2010 census put the number of Americans who are 18 or over at 234,564,071.[93] Politics of transgender bathrooms aside, we are making law based on the impact of a *group* of 1.4 million people on 233,164,071 individuals, about 0.6 percent of the American population.

If the debate were over whether transgender people were allowed to *use* public restrooms, the 1.4 million win every time. But there is no move to prevent them from entering public restrooms; the debate is over which public restrooms they are allowed to enter. Transgender Americans claim that "separate but equal" restroom facilities are inherently discriminatory as were separate but equal restrooms for "colored" during segregation. This is classic false equivalence. First of all, segregation required separate but equal facilities for blacks in every aspect of life: lunch counters, drinking fountains, bathrooms, etc. No one is telling transgender people they can't sit at certain lunch counters or drink from certain fountains. The only issue is bathrooms, and "junk in the trunk" is hardly equivalent to skin color.

I'm not one who fears transgender women will molest little girls in public restrooms, but I don't care to expose my five year old daughter to male anatomy until I'm ready to discuss it. I happen to believe that sex and childlike innocence are not compatible, and that it does not serve my daughter or the larger society to sexualize aspects of her world too early. The trans lobby insists that being transgender has nothing to do with sex, but when it comes to teaching my children about "private parts," I want to be the one who makes that determination.

There is also the issue of what age she is capable of understanding the anatomy lesson. There's a reason public schools wait until 5th grade to hold sex education classes. Some five year olds may be ready for the anatomy lesson, which individual parents should have the right to determine. Likewise, individual parents should have the right to determine that their little one is not.

Western culture supports individual parents making individual decisions for individual children as long as they don't impinge on the rights of others. Losing Western culture means the government makes those decisions for all of us.

Reason

Without the ability to share ideas freely and debate the merits of an argument, what do we have? We have the government telling us what's what with no opt-out button.

There are so many examples, but I'll limit myself to two.

Climate Science

They tell us that climate science is settled, but if it is, why isn't it? Nobody questions a sun-centered solar system because it is settled science. And it didn't settle because some government somewhere said so. The Catholic Church can say what it wants, but that doesn't obligate non-Catholic citizens to agree. Because scientists had the freedom to study the solar system, the science was settled soon enough. With climate science, we're expected to take it on faith—no further debate or scientific inquiry—that it is what the left says it is. What are people so afraid of that they have to shut down debate about it? And if I hear one more time the bogus statistic that 97 percent of all scientists believe in man-made global warming, I really will pop a gasket.

In 2015, President Obama tweeted,[94] "Ninety-seven percent of scientists agree: Climate change is real, man-made and dangerous." and "Read more" with a link to a Reuters piece about the new gold standard of anthropogenic global warming (AGW) studies.[95] (As an aside, can we really trust the judgment of someone who writes out "ninety-seven percent" on Twitter when "97%" is only three of the allotted 140 characters? Just sayin'.)

The new "everybody's using it" study was done by John Cook of the University of Queensland in Australia.[96] It is cited by everyone from President Obama to NASA.[97] The Cook study was criticized by Richard J. Tol of Sussex University[98] who was himself subsequently criticized by Cook. [99] I'm not a climate scientist, but I did blow up my organic chem lab at Berkeley, and I can read English.

- In the Cook study, 66.4 percent of the abstracts looked at did not explicitly state a position on AGW and were not included in the results.

- Tol points out in his critique of Cook that were the 66.4 percent of abstracts included, it would reduce the consensus to 33-63 percent.

- Cook points out in his critique of Tol's critique of him that no explicit position taken means nothing in a field where science is settled. Scientists don't take explicit positions on a heliocentric solar system because nobody questions it.

Cook's methodology of excluding the "no position" abstracts make sense if the science is settled. So why are there still so many scientists who say it isn't? I'm not settled on it being settled, but what do I know? I do notice something peculiar, however: only in studies on climate change are there *political* points made.

From Cook's 2013 study:

> *The public perception of a scientific consensus on AGW is a necessary element in public support for climate policy (Ding et al 2011). However, there is a significant gap between public perception and reality, with 57% of the US public either disagreeing or unaware that scientists overwhelmingly agree that the earth is warming due to human activity (Pew 2012). Contributing to this 'consensus gap' are campaigns designed to confuse the public about the level of agreement among climate scientists. In 1991, Western Fuels Association conducted a $510 000 campaign whose primary goal was to 'reposition global warming as the-*

*ory (not fact)'. A key strategy involved constructing the impression of active scientific debate using dissenting scientists as spokesmen (Oreskes 2010). **The situation is exacerbated by media treatment of the climate issue, where the normative practice of providing opposing sides with equal attention has allowed a vocal minority to have their views amplified** (Boykoff and Boykoff 2004).*[emphasis added]

Is that really science? Can a scientist who writes that be considered objective in evaluating science about climate change? And don't you think it's odd that if science is the god of climate change information, scientists would re-write science for political ends?

Scientists at the National Oceanic and Atmospheric Administration (NOAA) re-wrote climate science to eliminate evidence of the slowed rate of global temperature growth between 1998 and 2013.[100] Testifying before Congress, Dr. John Bates, the recently retired principal scientist at NOAA's National Climatic Data Center, said the re-write was used "to discredit the notion of a global warming hiatus and [a] rush to time the publication of the paper to influence national and international deliberations on climate policy." In other words, NOAA rushed to publish a landmark paper that exaggerated global warming and timed it to influence the Paris Agreement on climate change.

Intelligent Design

I know you're overly-impressed with my killer take-down of politically-motivated data, so I will spare you. I will even spare you the cookbook instructions for researching the topic yourself. Like I said, you have to take responsibility for your own intellectual journey at some point. I will suggest that you start with *On the Origin of Species* by Charles Darwin. Although his book is titled *On the Origin of Species*, Darwin never addresses the *origin* of species but rather their evolutionary adaptation over time.

(Before we go any further, it must be said that I don't have a dog in the creationism – evolution fight; I have a dog in the intellectual honesty fight.)

Abiogenesis is the theory that the first living speck of matter arose from non-living matter, which would be awesome if we could replicate it because then, who needs God? Darwin figured we would figure out how eventually. More than 150 years later, we still haven't. Individual scientists or groups put forth theories, breathlessly informing us that *we're almost there*, but with something as complex as abiogenesis, a miss is as good as a mile, *n'est-ce pas?*

Wiggle words that accompany theories of abiogenesis:

- "Several recent advances *suggest* that we *may be* getting close to creating life."[101] [emphasis added]
- "Science is now so close to constructing cells capable of reproduction from a feedstock of simple molecules that we have to acknowledge that it will eventually be done."[102]
- "Astrobiologists are collecting growing evidence that suggests life *may* have begun elsewhere in the galaxy and was carried here by meteorites or comets around 3.8 to 4 billion years ago - a theory known as panspermia."[103] [emphasis added]
- Understanding the thermodynamic function of life *may* shed light on its origin.... we *hypothesize* that life began, and persists today, as a catalyst for the absorption and dissipation of sunlight on the surface of Archean seas. The resulting heat *could* then be efficiently harvested by other irreversible processes such as the water cycle, hurricanes, and ocean and wind currents.[104] [emphasis added]

Any or all of these theories may be true. Call me when we really do figure it out, and by "figure it out," I mean replicate it in a lab. Until then, don't tell me the science gods have already determined the parameters of intellectual discourse on the origin of life

Freedom

The first casualty of our pull-back on teaching Western Civilization is our Constitution. The very first amendment—so I'm thinkin' it's probably kinda important—gives us the right of free speech:

Congress shall make no law respecting an establishment of religion, or prohibiting the free exercise thereof; or abridging the freedom of speech, or of the press; or the right of the people peaceably to assemble, and to petition the Government for a redress of grievances.

Are there any limits to our freedom of speech, you ask? As a matter of fact, there are. We all know you can't shout "fire" in a crowded theater. (If this is the first time you're hearing that, you have a bone to pick with your state's Department of Education.) Why can't we shout fire in a crowded theater?

In *Schenck v. United States*, the Supreme Court ruled that:[105]

Words which, ordinarily and in many places, would be within the freedom of speech protected by the First Amendment may become subject to prohibition when of such a nature and used in such circumstances as to create a clear and present danger that they will bring about the substantive evils which Congress has a right to prevent. The character of every act depends upon the circumstances in which it is done.

The operative words are "clear and present danger." You can't yell "fire" in a crowded theater because the stampede might kill a ticket-holder or two.

In *Chaplinsky v. New Hampshire*, the Supreme Court ruled that "fighting words," "which, by their very utterance, inflict injury or tend to incite an immediate breach of the peace" are not protected under the First Amendment.[106]

The best source of easily-digestible information on the First Amendment is the ACLU.[107] I have to give it to them for intellectual honesty and integrity. They emphatically negate the concept of "hate speech," which has to make them total pariahs at leftie dinner parties. I'm not sure how welcome they would be at rightie dinner parties either. Poor ACLU. They're probably very hungry.

The ACLU has often been at the center of controversy for defending the free speech rights of groups that spew hate, such as the Ku Klux Klan and the Nazis. But if only popular ideas were protected, we wouldn't need a First Amendment. History teaches that the first target of government repression is never the last. If we do not come to the defense of the free speech rights of the most unpopular among us, even if their views are antithetical to the very freedom the First Amendment stands for, then no one's liberty will be secure. In that sense, all First Amendment rights are "indivisible."

Censoring so-called hate speech also runs counter to the long-term interests of the most frequent victims of hate: racial, ethnic, religious and sexual minorities. We should not give the government the power to decide which opinions are hateful, for history has taught us that government is more apt to use this power to prosecute minorities than to protect them.

Unless I'm missing something, we have the freedom to offend each other, and thank goodness for that. But if that's the case, why do elite universities prohibit students offending each other? Because they can.

University Speech Codes

The Foundation for Individual Rights in Education (FIRE) defines a "speech code" as:

> ...any university regulation or policy that prohibits expression that would be protected by the First Amendment in society at large. Any policy—such as a harassment policy, a protest and demonstration policy, or an IT acceptable use policy—can be a speech code if it prohibits protected speech or expression."[108]

A random smattering of such codes includes:

Boston University – Prohibits the use of any computing facility to transmit "annoying" material.[109]

Chicago State University – Prohibits electronic communication that tends to "shed a negative light on any member of the community" and "otherwise unacceptable comments."[110]

DePauw University – Prohibits transmission of electronic communication that "promotes hate or violence."[111]

George Washington University – Prohibits "gender stereotyping and policing" (whatever that means) so that students do not feel "unsafe, targeted, or unable to go about their daily lives."[112]

Howard University – Prohibits verbal, electronic, visual, written, or physical behavior that "is likely to provoke or otherwise result in a negative or injurious response, mental or emotional distress." This includes "inflicting ... psychological or emotional harm" or "undue stress."[113]

Marquette University – Prohibits situations that "could result in mental, emotional or physical discomfort."[114]

Middlebury College – Prohibits "provoking remarks" about or relating to a student's or employee's sex or sexual orientation.[115] Also prohibits behavior that "demonstrates contempt for the generally accepted values of the intellectual community."[116]

Rice University – Prohibits transmission of unsolicited information that "panders to bigotry, sexism, or other forms of prohibited discrimination."[117]

Swarthmore College – Prohibits conduct that interferes with a person's "peaceful enjoyment of residence and community." Subject to disciplinary action, up to and including expulsion/dismissal.[118]

Why do elite universities bar conservative speakers or interfere with their exercise of free speech? Because they can. They can also make unreasonable demands as UC Berkeley did to Ann Coulter; or let protesters shut down the event as Middlebury College did to Charles Murray; or direct campus police to not interfere when protesters riot as Berkeley did to Milo Yiannopoulos.

Sometimes, they just let the students handle it. Two recent incidents both happened to Heather Mac Donald, Manhattan Institute Scholar and author of *The War on Cops*. Mac Donald was invited to UCLA on April 5, 2017 at the behest of the Bruin Republicans to give a Blue Lives Matter talk but was heckled, shouted down, and ultimately escorted off campus by police before she could finish. The next night, April 6, she was scheduled to give the same talk at Claremont McKenna, an institution that was, until recently, known for its conservatism.

At Claremont McKenna, protesters blocked the doors to the auditorium where Mac Donald was to speak, preventing all of the students who wanted to attend the lecture from getting in. Mac Donald was escorted by police to an empty lecture hall from which she live streamed the speech while demonstrators chanted, "Shut it down!" throughout the building. Organizers made sure to move the podium away from the windows lest the protesters discover where to find Mac Donald.[119]

As bad as the foregoing examples are, they all involve college administrators curtailing free speech on campus. How scary is it that now students are starting to assert themselves as the arbiters of acceptable speech before which college administrators must bow?

After the Mac Donald incident, Pomona College president David Oxtoby sent an email to the entire student body reiterating the college's commitment to free speech and academic freedom, a quite reasonable statement for a college president to make under the circumstances. Reasonable under a Western culture framework of intellectual inquiry, reason, and progress.

A few students, however, took him to task in an open letter.[120] It really must be read in its entirety:

Dear David Oxtoby,

We, few of the Black students here at Pomona College and the Claremont Colleges, would like to address several of the points made in your 'Academic Freedom and Free Speech' email sent out to the entire student body on April 7, 2017 in response to a student protest against Heather Mac Donald's talk at Claremont McKenna College's (CMC) Athenaeum. We believe that given your position as President of this institution your voice holds significant weight in campus discourse. That power comes with immense responsibility, especially when you could dictate campus culture, climate, and the alleged mission of this institution. As President, you are charged with upholding principles of Pomona College. Though this institution as well as many others including this entire country, have been founded upon the oppression and degradation of marginalized bodies, it has a liability to protect the students that it serves. The paradox is that Pomona's past is rooted in domination of marginalized peoples and communities and the student body has a significant population of students from these backgrounds. Your recent statement reveals where Pomona's true intentions lie.

Free speech, a right many freedom movements have fought for, has recently become a tool appropriated by hegemonic institutions. It has not just empowered students from marginalized backgrounds to voice their qualms and criticize aspects of the institution, but it has given those who seek to perpetuate systems of domination a platform to project their bigotry. Thus, if "our mission is founded upon the discovery of truth," how does free speech uphold that value? The notion of discourse, when it comes to discussions about experiences and identities, deters the 'Columbusing' of established realities and truths (coded as 'intellectual inquiry') that the institution promotes. Pomona cannot have its cake and eat it, too. Either you support students of marginalized identities, particularly Black students, or leave us to protect and organize for our communities without the impositions of your patronization, without your binary respectability politics, and without your monolithic perceptions of protest and organizing. In addition, non-Black individuals do not have the right to prescribe how Black people respond to anti-Blackness.

Your statement contains unnuanced views surrounding the academy and a belief in searching for some venerated truth. Historically, white supremacy has venerated the idea of objectivity, and wielded a dichotomy of 'subjectivity vs. objectivity' as a means of silencing oppressed peoples. The idea that there is a single truth--'the Truth'--is a construct of the Euro-West that is deeply rooted in the Enlightenment, which was a movement that also described Black and Brown people as both subhuman and impervious to pain. This construction is a myth and white supremacy, imperialism, colonization, capitalism, and the United States of America are all of its progeny. The idea that the truth is an entity for which we must search, in matters that endanger our abilities to exist in open spaces, is an attempt to silence oppressed peoples. We, Black students, exist with a myriad of different identities. We are queer, trans, differently-abled, poor/low-income, undocumented, Muslim, first-generation and/or immigrant, and positioned in different spaces across Africa and the African diaspora. The idea that we must subject ourselves routinely to the hate speech of fascists who want for us not to exist plays on the same Eurocentric constructs that believed Black people to be impervious to pain and apathetic to the brutal and violent conditions of white supremacy.

The idea that the search for this truth involves entertaining Heather Mac Donald's hate speech is illogical. If engaged, Heather Mac Donald would not be debating on mere difference of opinion, but the right of Black people to exist. Heather Mac Donald is a fascist, a white supremacist, a warhawk, a transphobe, a queerphobe, a classist, and ignorant of interlocking systems of domination that produce the lethal conditions under which oppressed peoples are forced to live. Why are you, and other persons in positions of power at these institutions, protecting a fascist and her hate speech and not students that are directly affected by her presence?

Advocating for white supremacy and giving white supremacists platforms wherefrom their toxic and deadly illogic may be disseminated is condoning violence against Black people. Heather Mac Donald does not have the right to an audience at the Athenaeum, a private venue wherefrom she received compensation. Dictating and condemning non-respectable forms of protest while parroting the phrase that "protest has a celebrated" place on campus is contradictory at best and anti-Black at worst.

This is not an argument rooted in Heather's loss of "free speech" or academic freedom. She is a well-known public figure, her views are well documented. Rather, our praxis is focused on not allowing her anti-Black platform to be legitimized in front of an audience, which she does not have the right to. Engaging with her, a white supremacist fascist supporter of the police state, is a form of violence.

Protest that doesn't disrupt the status quo is benign and doesn't function to overthrow systems of oppression, which is the ultimate goal.

To conclude our statement, we invite you to respond to this email by Tuesday, April 18, 2017 at 4:07pm (since we have more energy to expend on the frivolity of this institution and not Black lives). Also, we demand a revised email sent to the entire student body, faculty, and staff by Thursday, April 20, 2017, apologizing for the previous patronizing statement, enforcing that Pomona College does not tolerate hate speech and speech that projects violence onto the bodies of its marginalized students and oppressed peoples, especially Black students who straddle the intersection of marginalized identities, and explaining the steps the institution will take and the resources it will allocate to protect the aforementioned students.

This grammatically-tortured attack on Western culture is almost breathtaking in its scope. If I understand them correctly:

- They are black.
- They feel it their place to lecture a college president on how he upholds the college's principles.
- Speech is free for marginalized people but no one else.
- The world is divided into black and non-black individuals, one of whom (black) determines reality for everyone.
- Truth is a white supremacist concept designed to harm and silence any suckas who fall for it.
- The "myth" of objective truth spawned white supremacy, imperialism, colonialism, capitalism, and the United States of America (and probably a lot of other spawn of Satan they didn't have time to go into).
- If anyone says something they don't like, he or she is a fascist and wants to crush their existence.
- If they don't like what someone says, it is hate speech.
- Differences of opinion are code for debating the right of black people to exist.
- If someone holds a conservative opinion, he or she is a fascist, a white supremacist, a warhawk, a transphobe, a queerphobe, a classist, and an idiot who doesn't get the Victim Olympics. At all.
- They will not "legitimize" a conservative speaker by engaging with him or her because it would be a form of violence (to them).

Give those kids a degree! From a capitalist institution that is the "progeny" of American ideals and prosperity.

Faculty-to-Faculty Fascism

Professors at Wellesley—professors!—at Wellesley!—also take issue with the idea that speech is free in this country.[121] After a prominent feminist intellectual (but not the right kind of feminist because "white feminism isn't feminism"[122]) spoke on campus, the Faculty on Commission for Ethnicity, Race, and Equity (CERE) sent a letter of rebuke to the Wellesley Community of faculty and staff. It as well deserves to be read in its entirety:

> *To: Wellesley Community*
> *From: Faculty on Commission for Ethnicity, Race, and Equity (CERE)*
> *Re: Laura Kipnis visit and aftermath*
>
> *3/20/17*
>
> *Over the past few years, several guest speakers with controversial and objectionable beliefs have presented their ideas at Wellesley. We, the faculty in CERE, defend free speech and believe it is essential to a liberal arts education. However, as historian W. Jelani Cobb notes, "The freedom to offend the powerful is not equivalent to the freedom to bully the relatively disempowered. The enlightenment principles that undergird free speech also prescribed that the natural limits of one's liberty lie at the precise point at which it begins to impose upon the liberty of another." There is no doubt that the speakers in question impose on the liberty of students, staff, and faculty at Wellesley. We are especially concerned with the impact of speakers' presentations on Wellesley students, who often feel the injury most acutely and invest time and energy in rebutting the speakers' arguments. Students object*

in order to affirm their humanity. This work is not optional; students feel they would be unable to carry out their responsibilities as students without standing up for themselves. Furthermore, we object to the notion that onlookers who are part of the faculty or administration are qualified to adjudicate the harm described by students, especially when so many students have come forward. When dozens of students tell us they are in distress as a result of a speaker's words, we must take these complaints at face value. What is especially disturbing about this pattern of harm is that in many cases, the damage could have been avoided. The speakers who appeared on campus presented ideas that they had published, and those who hosted the speakers could certainly anticipate that these ideas would be painful to significant portions of the Wellesley community. Laura Kipnis's recent visit to Wellesley prompted students to respond to Kipnis's presentation with a video post on Facebook. Kipnis posted the video on her page, and professor Tom Cushman left a comment that publicly disparaged the students who produced the video. Professor Cushman apologized for his remarks, but in light of these developments, we recommend the following. First, those who invite speakers to campus should consider whether, in their zeal for promoting debate, they might, in fact, stifle productive debate by enabling the bullying of disempowered groups. We in CERE are happy to serve as a sounding board when hosts are considering inviting controversial speakers, to help sponsors think through the various implications of extending an invitation.

Second, standards of respect and rigor must remain paramount when considering whether a speaker is actually qualified for the platform granted by an invitation to Wellesley. In the case of an academic speaker, we ask that the Wellesley host not only consider whether the speaker holds credentials, but whether the presenter has standing in his/her/their discipline. This is not a matter of ideological bias. Pseudoscience suggesting that men are more naturally equipped to excel in STEM fields than women, for example, has no place at Wellesley. Similar arguments pertaining to race, ethnicity, sexuality, religion, and other identity markers are equally inappropriate. Third, faculty and administrators should step up in defense of themselves and all members of the Wellesley community. The responsibility to defend the disempowered does not rest solely with students, and the injuries suffered by students, faculty, and staff are not contained within the specific identity group in question; they ripple throughout our community and prevent Wellesley from living out its mission.

If I understand them correctly,

- Some beliefs are "objectionable," and they will decide which ones.
- Speech is free unless it hurts someone's feelings in a group they care about.
- Opposing opinions are a threat to liberty.
- Students are so injured by controversial ideas that they are unable to carry out their responsibilities as students.
- Students must object to controversial speakers in order to affirm their humanity (whatever that means).
- Faculty and administrators have no right to an opinion on the self-reported "harm" of students.
- If the university knows in advance that a speaker's words will be "painful" to some students, they have an obligation to prevent "distress."

- Controversial speakers might have a chilling effect on debate because college students in America can't be counted on to express themselves.
- They want to "help" other faculty think through what may happen if they invite certain controversial speakers. (Did the hair just go up on the back of your neck?)
- They will decide what science is and what it is not.
- Objective criteria like academic credentials don't count. Only speakers who don't tick anybody off, i.e., "have standing in his/her/their discipline," are approved.

Progress

Thirty years ago, if you graduated from Harvard Law School, you were locked and loaded for anything the criminal justice system might throw at you. If you graduate from Harvard today, or from a lot of other law schools for that matter, you better pray/hope/affirm that you never have to handle a sexual assault case—or more poignantly, that no one ever needs you to. Professors all over the country are deciding courses on rape law just aren't worth it.[123]

Why? The future attorneys of America are too delicate. How delicate, you ask? So delicate that rape law on an exam may traumatize them enough to impair their performance. So delicate that their tender ears can't hear the word "violate" fall from a professor's lips in reference to violations of the law. Students demand "trigger warnings" to protect themselves from experiencing discomfort and feel entitled to skip classes with material that might be upsetting.

Contrast the modern delicateness of today's elite college student with the grit of a soldier who stormed the beaches at Normandy in WWII. In June 1944, 29,000 Americans lost their lives in a single day. Can you imagine the trauma to those who lived to tell? Yet they came back from war—we called it shell shock back then—raised families, went to work, and never spoke of it again. At elite universities across the country today, students are traumatized by emotional injuries sustained during classroom conversations.

Until quite recently, we were expected to behave with a certain amount of decorum at public events. Oh, sure, Occupy Wall Street and the Women's March weren't held to such standards, but certainly graduates at their commencement ceremony were. Maybe it all started to go downhill in 2010 when Jon Stewart addressed President Obama as "dude." Until then, the worst thing that happened to conservative speakers was being disinvited to give commencement addresses. They weren't heckled, booed, shouted down, and given the back during the entire length of their speech. Bethune-Cookman University recently laid down fresh tracks in this area when Secretary of Education Betsy DeVos spoke to the graduating class of 2017.[124] I use the term "spoke" extremely loosely. It got so bad that Bethune-Cookman's president, Edison O. Jackson, stepped to the podium and announced, "If this behavior continues, your degrees will be mailed to you."

Three cheers for President Jackson. I honestly can't imagine any other college president having the spine to check such abominable behavior on the part of graduates at a commencement ceremony. I also admire Jackson for his defense of DeVos as his choice for commencement speaker. "I am of the belief that it does not benefit our students to suppress voices that we disagree with, or limit students to only those perspectives that are broadly sanctioned by a specific community."

How refreshing! Another voice of reason was the United Negro College Fund president and CEO who tweeted, "I believe we should hear Secretary DeVos at @bethunecookman, just as we want her and President Trump to hear the voices of #HBCUs."

Why, it's almost like civilized discourse goes hand in hand with reason, freedom, progress, and individualism!

Going Once, Going Twice...

Western culture isn't gone yet, but you can see the writing on the wall. We lose a little more of it every time we sacrifice our power as individuals for our status as a member of some group; every time we sacrifice our freedoms for some illusory warm fuzzies; every time we baby and coddle and excuse those who will be our future leaders and judges and parents; and every time we sacrifice reason for anything.

Key Points

- Two examples of what happens without a robust Western culture are a fundamental misunderstanding of our freedom of speech, and intolerance for politically incorrect scientific inquiry.
- Western culture is based on individualism, and one of the fastest way to kill it is to divide us into identity groups.
- Parents and college administrators are responsible for most of the entitlement attitude among undergraduates.
- When a college administrator puts a foot down, it works.
- People rise to the level of expectation for them. We're going backward if college students feel justified in turning their backs on a cabinet secretary at their commencement ceremony.

Your Mission,
Should You Choose to Accept It

I wrote this book as a love letter to America. My near-America death experience in my younger days makes me exquisitely aware of what I almost lost and what we as a society are in the midst of losing. We are a fragile experiment in the history of humanity, and, without careful tending, we will sink back into the bog of a culture without God-given rights, the Protestant work ethic, limitless imagination, and fierce and free independence.

There has never been another country in the world where no matter who you are, no matter what circumstances you're born into, you are free to rise above them. A commoner in Britain is always a commoner. A poor, fatherless, black kid in America can become president.

There has never been another country in the world with so much freedom and so much complexity at the same time. Sweden is great, but it's not America.

There is no other country in the world that has welcomed and absorbed so many people from so many other cultures. Next to our God-given rights, it is what is best about us. Ellis Island was the portal through which America became greater.

If you're an American, you have the luxury of paying no attention to what's going on in the world. Where much of the world is on fire with terror, you can go to the movies, grab a bite to eat, hang out with your friends, and never once give thought to young girls taken as Yazidi sex slaves. You can obsess over your hair or your weight or the car you drive. None of this is becoming to us, but it speaks to the luxury of safety and comfort we live in.

You can choose the life you want for yourself: marriage, career, kids, dogs, video games all day, or some combination. You can decide from minute to minute how you want to use your freedoms and opportunities. You get to decide whether to look on the bright side because there is a very bright side.

You have a cell phone, a refrigerator, indoor plumbing, and a color TV. If you take those things for granted, you only make my point. That would be the high life for most of the people in the world.

Do you want your children and grandchildren to have the same privilege of the same America you enjoy? It is fragile, this once in human history creation of ours. Complacency is its fruit and its curse. If we don't look up from *Game of Thrones,* we will cease to be the best of Western culture and not even know it's happening until it's too late. I have tried to be the erudite yet humorous Paul Revere sounding the alarm that the cracks in our foundation are coming, and many are already here.

It must be said that while some cracks are from ignorance or complacency, some cracks are deliberately encouraged. There are some very good people in this country who believe it needs to be fundamentally transformed. There are also some people who are evil and want to destroy it for the sake of destruction. But make no mistake, this is a pitched battle.

So what can you do? Be knowledgeable, be bold, be fearless, be American.

Be Knowledgeable

Remember the cardinal rule of knowledge: Don't believe it until you've verified it for yourself. When I started verifying information before I wrote about it, I cringed to realize how many times I had, in all innocence, spread false information. I would wager that 90 percent of what you hear or read that is false is being innocently spread by people like my former self who are unaware that it's false.

The best way to verify something is to go straight to the source. If you read an article about FBI crime statistics, click on the link to the FBI's website. Check it out. You'll know whether the information in the article is accurate or whether someone is simply repeating someone else's (faulty) interpretation of FBI stats. If the article says it's based on FBI crime stats but doesn't link out to the FBI site, that's a red flag.

Get your news from opposite ends of the political spectrum.

The most decent of us have unconscious biases that filter what we read and watch and hear. That's just the way it is; there's no cure possible. If you get your information from only one segment of the political spectrum, you won't even recognize your biases. Just like fish don't know they're wet because they're never dry. There's nothing wrong with consciously choosing the filter you use in life, but let the choice be informed. Know what your filter is before you give it the power to frame your world.

I watch Tucker Carlson on Fox and I watch Van Jones on CNN. I read National Review and the Federalist, and I read Salon and Mother Jones (only occasionally, I must admit, although I had a subscription to Mother Jones in college and remember it fondly as a very good read). I read the New York Times, and I read the Wall Street Journal editorial page. I follow lefties and righties on Twitter and a lot of other in-betweens.

I know what my filter is, and I'm quite happy with it, but I keep it humble in case I encounter information that requires an adjustment. Like when I fact check something I'm already sure of and find out I was dead wrong. "If you're never wrong, you're not doing it right" is my motto. You can be right all the time if you enjoy echo chambers, but don't kid yourself that your knowledge is robust.

Pick one issue you're really interested in and read more deeply about it.

If you read a handful of articles about the same issue, you'll realize there's not much originality out there. In other words, it's not that hard to get your knowledge up to speed. Just plunge in. It won't be long before you've read the same history, politics, and social ramifications of an issue so many times that you'll have it down. Then it's pretty straightforward to keep up with new developments and information.

The other cool thing you'll realize is that everything is connected to everything else. You can't learn about incarceration rates without picking up some knowledge about crime, law enforcement, race relations, public safety, illegal immigration, gangs, jailhouse conversions, and neck tattoos. Without even trying!

Respect that others have different filters.

We are a product of our life experience. We can't step outside of it, and it drives every thought we have and every choice we make.

As a child of the 70s, raised in suburban California by middle class parents with white collar jobs, I feel safer when I see the police. A millennial raised in Chicago by a single mom in public housing may feel less safe when he sees the police. Those of us who feel safer when we see the police think it's so obvious what everyone should do if they get stopped: Do what the cops tell you. Don't run. That works in the rational part of your mind. But if you have been taught your whole life (wrongly) that the police are your enemy, you are in survival mode when you see them, and nothing about that is rational. Imagine if you were pulled over by a Grizzly bear. It wouldn't matter what people told you to do. You would be in fight-or-flight. It's the irrational primitive part of the brain that operates when we're terrified.

Putting yourself in someone else's shoes doesn't change anything, but it helps you see why he sees the world the way he does. Now, if he could just do the same for you, we could all sing kumbaya and go home.

Talk about the issue, preferably to your kids

Nothing cements understanding in your mind like talking about it, and teaching a young person about it is even better. When it comes to kids, it's really tempting to communicate about issues with a "thus I spake" attitude. If it works for you, go for it. But I figure my kids will encounter a lot of different opinions out there so I like to give them a chance to think about the issue in advance. We talk about different points of view people can have on a subject, for example, gay marriage. I tell them why I believe the way I do and suggest why someone else might believe differently. I tell them, "You get to decide for yourself what you think." They're going to anyway. You might as well send them on their way with a little love pat.

Be Bold

Are you a man or a mouse? And how important is this Western culture thing to you? I assume if you're reading this book, you care about preserving it. You can't do that unless you boldly go where you have not gone before. If what we were already doing was working, we wouldn't be watching Western culture slip away. To preserve it, we need to step up our game.

Only you know what comfort zone you're in right now. Whatever it is, push it a little bit. The idea is to be "ambassadors" for Western culture. And remember Jesse Jackson's admonition about not getting rid of Western culture but adding more voices to it. You're not out there crushing other cultures, you're simply bringing well-behaved Western culture to the party and showing it off a little bit. And do it with a little sass and courage; it's nothing to be ashamed of.

Be Fearless

You know you're going to get blowback in some circles if you promote/defend/explain/enjoy Western culture. Maybe a lot of it. I know I do, but thanks to my mentor, Taylor Swift and "Shake It Off," I'm ready. Whatever comes my way, I shake it off and enjoy myself to the hilt while doing it.

To paraphrase:

People say rotten things about me, but they don't know me, it's just what they say. It doesn't stop me because I have something bigger and better than being popular. It's going to be all right. I'm just going to shake it off.

If you can add a sense of humor, so much the better. It's actually fun once you get the hang of it. My favorite way to use it is responding to mean comments about my published articles. My favorite so far:

Mean person: *"Donna Carol Voss is a Berkeley grad, a former pagan, a Mormon on purpose, and an original thinker on twenty-first century living."* [from my contributor bio] *So, first this silly woman was in a pagan cult now she's in a Mormon tribe.*

And that qualifies her to write about ISIS how? DONNA! You need to get back to your Tupperware party!
    Me: *You're a little behind the curve. It's all about Norwex now.*

Just have fun with it and shake it off.

Be American

If you're a citizen of this country, you're an American. It doesn't matter where you came from or what you look like. You're an American because America is an idea. It's a set of values found nowhere else in the world to this degree. It's essentially freedom. Freedom of speech, freedom of religion, freedom of assembly, freedom of the press. Freedom, freedom, freedom, freedom.

So I can't tell you how to be American because being American means being free to be who you are. Only you can do you. Be you, and bring what you have to the table.

Be knowledgeable, be bold, be fearless, and be American. Don't take what we have for granted, or we won't have it for very long.

Hey hey, ho ho, Western culture, we're not about to let you go.

Acknowledgment

As corny as it sounds, I want to acknowledge America. I feel so lucky to be an American; I give thanks for it every day. We might be a mess, but we're *my* mess. Just like you can talk bad about your family but no one else can, I can criticize and defend us all at the same time. Whatever we fail, we are the freest country ever to have existed on earth. No one can take that away from us.

Freedom is our mother tongue. It is the alpha and omega, the First Principle that undergirds every other in our Constitution. When we struggle against our sins, flaws, and injustices, we're struggling *for* freedom. We're struggling to free every last one of us from the man-made barriers that block our fulfillment of inalienable, God-given rights: life, liberty, and the pursuit of happiness.

You don't have to be religious to appreciate rights bestowed by our Creator. You can understand that to mean simply that they are rights inherent in you as an American, and that they cannot be taken away.

Cannot. Be. Taken. Away.

Those words are revolutionary in concept, miraculous in practice, and desperately vulnerable to complacency. Because they're ideals. Not guarantees.

I want to acknowledge America because I take none of this for granted. The older I get, the more amazed and grateful I am. I want to acknowledge every generation of Americans—good, bad, and ugly—who have preserved and passed on what is essential about us.

I want to acknowledge that it's an honor and a privilege to be an American.

Endnotes

Hey Hey, Ho Ho, Western Culture, Please Don't Go

1   "Jesse Jackson Didn't Lead Chant Against Western Culture," letter to the editor, *Chronicle of Higher Education*, November 21, 2016, http://www.chronicle.com/blogs/letters/jesse-jackson-didnt-lead-chant-against-western-culture/.

2   Rod Nordland, "Taliban and Government Imperil Gains for Afghan Women, Advocates Say," *New York Times*, February 7, 2014, https://www.nytimes.com/2014/02/08/world/asia/womens-rights-seen-as-vulnerable-to-reversal-in-afghanistan.html.

3   Gustavo Ocando, "Hungry Venezuelans killing flamingos and anteaters for food, biologists say," *Miami Herald*, February 10, 2017, http://www.miami-herald.com/news/nation-world/world/americas/venezuela/article131778819.html.

4   Robert Rapier, "Venezuela's Oil Reserves Are Probably Vastly Over-stated," *Forbes*, July 1, 2016, https://www.forbes.com/sites/rrapier/2016/07/01/venezuelas-oil-reserves-are-probably-vastly-overstated/#5be87b2f4497.

5   Instead of investing profits back into further development of the reserves—the most basic idea of Capitalism 101—the government siphoned money off for other things. Despite the significant rise in its recoverable oil post-Western investment, Venezuela's production of crude oil dropped 20 percent over the last decade. (During that same decade, US oil production rose more than 80 percent.) Venezuela still has a boatload of oil, but it is unrecoverable without outside investment, and you flunk Capitalism 101 if you burn your investors. Not only are ConocoPhillips and ExxonMobil out, so is every other Western oil company who saw what happened to them.

Back in the Day, Western Civ Was Cool

6   Amanda Ruggeri, "Beijing's Extraordinary Grand Canal," *BBC Travel,* October 2, 2014, http://www.bbc.com/travel/story/20140930-beijings-extraordinary-grand-canal.

7   Herodotus, *The History*, trans. David Grene (Chicago & London: University of Chicago Press), 2:19.

8   James Hannam, *The Genesis of Science: How the Christian Middle Ages Launched the Scientific Revolution* (Washington DC: Regnery, 2011), 83-100.

9   Rodney Stark, *How the West Won: The Neglected Story of the Triumph of Modernity,* (Delaware: ISI, 2015), 70-74.

10   Sarah Pruitt, "6 Reasons the Dark Ages Weren't So Dark," *History*, May 31, 2016, http://www.history.com/news/history-lists/6-reasons-the-dark-ages-werent-so-dark.

11   *Oxford Dictionary of Islam,* s.v. "Rightly Guided Caliphs," accessed April 13, 2017, http://www.oxfordislamicstudies.com/article/opr/t125/e2018.

12   Sayyid Muhammad Rizvi, "How did Islam Spread? By Sword or By Conversion?" *Al-Islam,* 2006, https://www.al-islam.org/articles/how-did-islam-spread-sword-or-conversion-sayyid-muhammad-rizvi.

13   N. Akmal Ayyubi, "Contribution of Al-Khwarizmi to Mathematics and Geography, *Muslim Heritage* (online education community of Muslims and non-Muslims), http://www.muslimheritage.com/article/contribution-al-khwarizmi-mathematics-and-geography.

14   Tony Abboud, *Al-Kindi: Father of Arab Philosophy (Great Muslim Philosophers and Scientists of the Middle Ages,* (New York: Rosen), 38; Mohaini Mohamed, *Great Muslim Mathematicians,* (Malaysia: Penerbit, 2000), 19; George Gheverghese Joseph, *The Crest of the Peacock: Non-European Roots of Mathematics (Third Edition),* (Princeton: Princeton University, 2011), 455.

15   J.J. O'Connor and E.F. Robertson, "Abu Ja'far Muhammad ibn Musa Al-Khwarizmi," *MacTutor History of Mathematics Archive*, School of Mathematics

and Statistics, University of St. Andrews, Scotland, http://www-history.mcs.st-and.ac.uk/Biographies/Al-Khwarizmi.html.

16   K.E. Carr, "Islamic Mathematics," *Quatr.us,* April 2016, http://quatr.
us/islam/science/math.htm.

17   Marshall G.S. Hodgson, *Rethinking World History: Essays on Europe, Islam and World History (Studies in Comparative World History),* ed. Michael Adas and Edmund Burke III and Philip D. Curtin, (Cambridge: Cambridge University, 1993), 190.

18   The Scholar Robert Pasnau, "The Islamic Scholar Who Gave Us Modern Philosophy," *Humanities,* November/December 2011 |Volume 32, Number 6, https://www.neh.gov/humanities/2011/novemberdecember/feature/the-islamic-scholar-who-gave-us-modern-philosophy.

19   Bassam Tibi, *The Challenge of Fundamentalism: Political Islam and the New World Disorder,* (Berkeley-Los Angeles, University of California, 2002), 71.

20   Hillel Ofek, "Why the Arabic World Turned Away from Science," *The New Atlantis,* Number 30, Winter 2011, 3-23, http://www.thenewatlantis.com/publications/why-the-arabic-world-turned-away-from-science.

Western Culture Is Messy, I Can't Lie

21   Rodney Stark, *How the West Won: The Neglected Story of the Triumph of Modernity* (Wilmington: ISI Books, 2014), Kindle edition.

22   Karen L. Privat and Tamsin C. O'Connell, "Stable Isotope Analysis of Human and Faunal Remains from the Anglo-Saxon Cemetery at Berinsfield, Oxfordshire: Dietary and Social Implications," *Journal of Archaeological Science* (2002) 29, 779–790, doi:10.1006/jasc.2001.0785.

23   Howard W. French, "Cape Coast Journal; On Slavery, Africans Say the Guilt Is Theirs, Too," *New York Times,* December 27, 1994, http://www.nytimes.com/1994/12/27/world/cape-coast-journal-on-slavery-africans-say-the-guilt-is-theirs-too.html.

24   *The National Archives,* s.v. "Africa and the Caribbean: West Africa before the Europeans," accessed April 24, 2017, http://www.nationalarchives.gov.uk/pathways/blackhistory/africa_caribbean/west_africa.htm.

25   "Europeans Come to Western Africa," *KPBS,* accessed May 18, 2017, http://www.pbs.org/wgbh/aia/part1/1narr1.html.

26   *Encyclopaedia Britannica Online,* s.v. "Benin, Historical Kingdom, West Africa," accessed April 24, 2017, https://www.britannica.com/place/Benin-historical-kingdom-West-Africa.

27   It is estimated that Benin sold more than three million slaves to white exporters, for which Benin has apologized. See "Benin Officials Apologize for Role in U.S. Slave Trade," *Chicago Tribune,* May 1, 2000, http://articles.chicagotribune.com/2000-05-01/news/0005010158_1_slave-trade-benin-president-mathieu-kerekou.

28   See David Oshinsky, *Worse than Slavery: Parchman Farm and the Ordeal of Jim Crow Justice* (New York: Free Press, 1997).

29   There are so many more dark parts to our underbelly, but discussing each one is beyond the scope of this book. Nothing comes close to the heinousness of slavery, and I chose to focus on this evil to illustrate my point.

America Is the Worst Country There Is—Except for All the Others

30   "Dying to defend the planet: why Latin America is the deadliest place for environmentalists," *The Economist,* February 11, 2017, http://www.economist.com/news/americas/21716687-commodities-technology-and-bad-policing-why-latin-america-deadliest-place.

31   Radhika Sanghani, "The horrific story of Korea's 'comfort women' — forced to be sex slaves during World War Two," *The Telegraph,* December 29, 2015, http://www.telegraph.co.uk/women/life/the-horrific-story-of-koreas-comfort-women---forced-to-be-sex-sl/.

32   "India's Dalits still fighting untouchability," *BBC News,* June 27, 2012, http://www.bbc.com/news/world-asia-india-18394914.

33   "World Report 2016: Russia - Palliative Care," *Human Rights Watch,* https://www.hrw.org/world-report/2016/country-chapters/russia.

34   Female genital mutilation/cutting (FGM/C) refers to "all procedures involving partial or total removal of the female external genitalia or other injury to the female genital organs for non-medical reasons," *UNICEF,* December 2013, http://data.unicef.org/wp-content/uploads/country_profiles/Somalia/FGMC_SOM.pdf.

35   "World Report 2016 – China," *Human Rights Watch,* https://www.hrw.org/world-report/2016/country-chapters/china-and-tibet.

36   "Annual Report on the Death Penalty 2016," *Iran Human Rights,* April 3, 2017, https://iranhr.net/media/files/Rapport_iran_2016-GB-280317-BD.pdf.

37   "2009 Annual Report: Executions Highest in 10 Years," Iran Human Rights, March 10, 2009, https://iranhr.net/en/reports/7/.

38   "World Report 2016: Cuba – Arbitrary Detention and Short-Term Imprisonment," *Human Rights Watch,* https://www.hrw.org/world-report/2016/country-chapters/cuba#3159b0.

39   Julien Harneis, UNICEF Representative in Yemen, *Statement to UNICEF,* June 16, 2015, https://www.unicef.org/media/media_82280.html.

40   "World Report 2016 – Yemen," *Human Rights Watch,* https://www.hrw.org/world-report/2016/country-chapters/yemen#f4d4fe.

41   United States Committee on International Religious Freedom. (2017). "2017 annual report." Retrieved from http://www.uscirf.gov/sites/default/files/2017.USCIRFAnnualReport.pdf.

42   "World Health Statistics – 2016," *World Health Organization,* http://www.who.int/gho/publications/world_health_statistics/en/.

43   "The World Health Report 2000 – Health Systems: Improving

Performance," *World Health Organization*, pp. 152-155, http://www.who.int/whr/2000/en/whr00_en.pdf.

44   "2017 World Press Freedom Index," *Reporters Without Borders*, https://rsf.org/en/ranking/2017.

45   "Freedom of the Press," *Freedom House* (2016), https://freedomhouse.org/report/freedom-press/freedom-press-2016.

46   "RSF Survey 2016," *Reporters Without Borders,* https://rsf.org/sites/default/files/rsf_survey_en.pdf.

47   United States Census Bureau. (2016). *Census Bureau Releases 2016 Determinations for Section 203 of the Voting Rights Act* [Press release]. Retrieved from https://www.census.gov/newsroom/press-releases/2016/cb16-205.html.

48   "Freedom of the Press 2016 Methodology," *Freedom of the Press*, https://freedomhouse.org/report/freedom-press-2016-methodology.

49   Lennart Weibull, Anna Maria Jönsson and Ingela Wadbring, "Media Landscapes: Sweden," *European Journalism Centre*, accessed April 27, 2017, http://ejc.net/media_landscapes/sweden.

50   Daniel J. Mitchell, "The Laffer Curve Shows That Tax Increases Are a Very Bad Idea—Even if They Generate More Tax Revenue," *Forbes*, April 15, 2012, https://www.forbes.com/sites/danielmitchell/2012/04/15/the-laffer-curve-shows-that-tax-increases-are-a-very-bad-idea-even-if-they-generate-more-tax-revenue.

51   The Dental and Pharmaceutical Benefits Agency Database (accessed April 28, 2017), http://www.tlv.se/beslut/sok/lakemedel/.

52   Xiao-Ping Yang and Jane F. Reckelhoff, "Estrogen, hormonal replacement therapy and cardiovascular disease," *Current Opinion in Nephrology and Hypertension* 20, no. 2 (2011): 133-138. doi:10.1097/MNH.0b013e3283431921.

53   L. Lindh-Åstrand et al., "Hormone therapy might be underutilized in women with early onset menopause," *Human Reproduction* 30, no. 4 (2015): 848-852. doi:10.1093/humrep/dev017.

54   "BRCA1 and BRCA2: Cancer Risk and Genetic Testing," *National Cancer Institute*, accessed April 28, 2017, https://www.cancer.gov/about-cancer/causes-prevention/genetics/brca-fact-sheet#q2.

55   "U.S. and SEER Death Rates by Primary Cancer Site and Race/Ethnicity, 2010-2014," *National Institutes of Health*, accessed April, 28 2017, https://seer.cancer.gov/csr/1975_2014/results_single/sect_01_table.21_2pgs.pdf.

56   "Statistical Database on Cancer (English)," *The National Board of Health and Welfare*, Accessed April 28, 2017, http://www.socialstyrelsen.se/statistics/statisticaldatabase/cancer.

57   "Best ADHD medication," *Consumer Reports*, March 2012, http://www.consumerreports.org/cro/2012/03/best-treatments-for-children-with-adhd/index.htm.

58   Alexis de Tocqueville. 2002. *Democracy in America*. Translated and edited by Harvey C. Mansfield and Delba Winthrop. Chicago: University of Chicago Press, 127.

59   Alexis de Tocqueville. 1831. *Letters from America*. Translated by Frederick Brown. The Hudson Review, http://hudsonreview.com/2013/03/letters-from-america/#.WQgcxojyvBU.

60   Andre Jardin. 1989. *Tocqueville: A Biography*. Translated by Lydia Davis with Robert Hemenway. New York: Farrar, Straus, and Giroux, 118.

People Are Equal; Cultures Are Not

61   "The First in the Indies," *National Humanities Center*, http://nationalhumanitiescenter.org/pds/amerbegin/settlement/text1/ColumbusHispaniola.pdf.

62   "Magna Carta Translation," *National Archives and Records Administration*, translated by Nicholas Vincent, https://www.archives.gov/files/press/press-kits/magna-carta/magna-carta-translation.pdf.

63   "The English Bill of Rights 1689," *The Avalon Project – Yale Law School*, http://avalon.law.yale.edu/17th_century/england.asp.

64   Gustavo Ocando, "Hungry Venezuelans killing flamingos and anteaters for food, biologists say," *Miami Herald*, February 10, 2017, http://www.miamiherald.com/news/nation-world/world/americas/venezuela/article131778819.html.

65   "Orbital Maneuvering Systems," *NASA*, https://science.ksc.nasa.gov/shuttle/technology/sts-newsref/sts-oms.html#sts-oms.

66   "Members of Apollo 13 Team Reflect on 'NASA's Finest Hour,'" *NASA*, https://www.nasa.gov/content/members-of-apollo-13-team-reflect-on-nasas-finest-hour.

We Can Be Forgiven for Our Sins

67   *Encyclopedia Britannica Online*, s.v. "University," accessed May 6, 2017, https://www.britannica.com/topic/university.

68   Theology is not the practice of organized religion, and organized religion is not theology. The Roman Catholic Church at the end of the Middle Ages was based on a rational God and the ability to progress in our knowledge of him and his creation. But it was organized as an empire that rejected individualism.

69   *LDS Bible Dictionary* (1979), s.v. "repentance," 760.

70   Anshel Pfeffer and Shahar Ilan, "Speaking in German, Merkel Gets Standing Ovation in Knesset," *Haaretz*, March 19, 2008, http://www.haaretz.com/israel-news/speaking-in-german-merkel-gets-standing-ovation-in-knesset-1.241816.

71   Cherokee Nation v. Georgia, 30 U.S. 1 (1831).

72   James Van Ness, Esq., "The Federal Trust Doctrine—Realizing Chief Justice Marshall's Vision," *U.S. Department of the Interior*, accessed May 6, 2017, https://www.doi.gov/pmb/cadr/programs/native/gtgworkshop/The-Federal-Trust-Doctrine.

73   Shawn Regan, "5 Ways the Government Keeps Native Americans in Poverty," *Forbes*, March 13, 2014, https://www.forbes.com/sites/realspin/2014/03/13/5-ways-the-government-keeps-native-americans-in-poverty/#202680e32c27.

74   "Transcript of the Testimony of Paula Deen," *Lisa T. Jackson v. Paula Deen, et al.*, May 17, 2013, 22-23, http://www.cnn.com/interactive/2013/06/entertainment/deen-deposition/.

75   Michael Rothman, "Paula Deen and Lisa Jackson Reach Settlement," *ABC News*, August 23, 2013, http://abcnews.go.com/Entertainment/paula-deen-lisa-jackson-reach-settlement/story?id=20051341.

76   Orla Borg, "How a Danish Former Biker Turned Jihadist, then Double-Agent, Says he Helped the CIA Track and Kill Anwar Al Awlaki," *Public Radio International*, February 12, 2013, interview with Marco Werman, https://www.pri.org/stories/2013-02-12/how-danish-former-biker-turned-jihadist-then-double-agent-says-he-helped-cia.

Nobody Wins at the Victim Olympics

77   Katharine Q. Seelye and Abby Goodnough, "Candidate for Senate Defends Past Hiring," *New York Times*, April 30, 2012, http://www.nytimes.com/2012/05/01/us/politics/elizabeth-warrens-ancestry-irrelevant-in-hiring-law-schools-say.html.

78   For some of the pros and cons about affirmative action, see "Should affirmative action policies, which give preferential treatment based on minority status, be eliminated?" BalancedPolitics.org, last updated January 7, 2012, accessed May 13, 2017, https://www.balancedpolitics.org/affirmative_action.htm.

79   Mark Kantrowitz, "The Distribution of Grants and Scholarships by Race." Policy analysis for FinAid, September 2, 2011, http://www.finaid.org/scholarships/20110902racescholarships.pdf.

80   Cora Daniels et al, "50 Best Companies for Minorities," *Fortune*, June 28, 2004, http://archive.fortune.com/magazines/fortune/fortune_archive/2004/06/28/374393/index.htm.

81   Regents of University of California v. Bakke, 438 U.S. 265 (1978).

82   Linda Greenhouse is the Senior Research Scholar in Law, Knight Distinguished Journalist in Residence, and Joseph Goldstein Lecturer in Law at Yale Law School.

83   Linda Greenhouse, "The Supreme Court's Diversity Dilemma," *New York Times*, December 24, 2015, https://www.nytimes.com/2015/12/24/opinion/the-supreme-courts-diversity-dilemma.html.

84   *Urban Dictionary Online*, s.v. "get served," accessed May 15, 2017, http://www.urbandictionary.com/define.php?term=get%20served.

85   Jedidah C. Isler, "The 'Benefits' of Black Physics Students," *New York Times*, December 17, 2015, https://www.nytimes.com/2015/12/17/opinion/the-benefits-of-black-physics-students.html.

86   Fisher v. University of Texas, 579 U.S. ___ (2016).

87   Fisher v. University of Texas, Supreme Court case 14-981, oral arguments, December 9, 2015, transcript page 55, lines 16-23, https://www.supreme-court.gov/oral_arguments/argument_transcripts/14-981_p8k0.pdf.

88   *The Civil War Home Page*, "Results from the 1860 Census," accessed May 15, 2017, http://www.civil-war.net/pages/1860_census.html.

89   Laura Parson, "Are STEM Syllabi Gendered? A Feminist Critical Discourse Analysis" *The Qualitative Report* 21(1), 102-116. Retrieved from http://nsuworks.nova.edu/tqr/vol21/iss1/9.

90   Shelby Steele, *Shame: How America's Past Sins Have Polarized Our Country* (New York: Basic, 2015), 32.

91   "Organizing. Strategizing. Taking-Action. Deconstructing the Culture of White Supremacy and Privilege: Creating Peace, Equity and Opportunity in the Heartland," White Privilege Conference, Kansas City, Missouri, April 27 – April 30, 2017, http://www.whiteprivilegeconference.com/.

What We Lose if We Lose Western Culture

92   Andrew R. Flores et al, *How Many Adults Identify as Transgender in the United States*, The Williams Institute, June 2016, https://williamsinstitute.law.ucla.edu/wp-content/uploads/How-Many-Adults-Identify-as-Transgender-in-the-United-States.pdf.

93   Lindsay M. Howden and Julie A. Meyer, *Age and Sex Composition: 2010*, U.S. Census Bureau, May 2011, https://www.census.gov/prod/cen2010/briefs/c2010br-03.pdf.

94   President Barack Obama, *Twitter*, May 16, 2015, https://twitter.com/barackobama/status/335089477296988160?lang=en.

95   Alister Doyle, "Scientists say united on global warming, at odds with public view," Reuters, May 15, 2013, http://www.reuters.com/article/us-climate-scientists-idUSBRE94F00020130516#13uroi2ee8ifgVbh.97.

96   Cook et al, "Quantifying the consensus on anthropogenic global warming in the scientific literature," *Environmental Research Letters*, 8 024024 (2013), doi:10.1088/1748-9326/8/2/024024.

97   "Scientific Consensus: Earth's Climate is Warming," *NASA*, Accessed May 10, 2017, https://climate.nasa.gov/scientific-consensus/.

98   Richard Tol, "Comment on 'Quantifying the consensus on anthropogenic global warming in the scientific literature,'" *Environmental Research Letters*, 11 048001 (2016): doi:10.1088/1748-9326/11/4/048001.

99   Ibid.

100   US Congressional Committee on Science, Space, and Technology. (2017). *Former NOAA Scientist Confirms Colleagues Manipulated Climate Records* [Press release]. Retrieved from https://science.house.gov/news/press-releases/former-noaa-scientist-confirms-colleagues-manipulated-climate-records.

101   "The Origin of Life: abiotic synthesis of organic molecules," *Kimball's*

loads/2015/08/20040000/Computer-Usage-Policy-_-Information-Technolo-gy-Division-_-Chicago-State-University.pdf.

111   DePauw University, *Electronic Communications and Acceptable Use Policy*, January 7, 2006, 48, https://d28htnjz2elwuj.cloudfront.net/wp-content/uploads/2015/05/07072301/acceptable-use.pdf.

112   GW – Haven, *Sexual Harassment*, accessed May 10, 2017, https://d28htnjz2elwuj.cloudfront.net/wp-content/uploads/2016/09/20070330/gw-sex-ual-harassment.pdf.

113   Howard University, *Student Code of Conduct: Harassment*, accessed May 10, 2017, https://d28htnjz2elwuj.cloudfront.net/wp-content/up-loads/2003/04/22000000/conduct-code.pdf.

114   Marquette University, *Policies and Procedures: Sexual Misconduct Policy*, October 20, 2016, https://d28htnjz2elwuj.cloudfront.net/wp-content/uploads/2015/10/28151145/Marquette-University-Title-IX-Sexual-Harass-ment-Discrimination-and-Sexual-Misconduct-Policy-_-Policies-and-Procedu-res-_-Office-of-Student-Development-_-Marquette-University.pdf.

115   Middlebury College, *Anti-Harassment/Discrimination Policy*, June 6, 2016, http://www.middlebury.edu/about/handbook/misc/antiharassment.

116   Middlebury College, *General Conduct Standards*, August 25, 2016, https://d28htnjz2elwuj.cloudfront.net/wp-content/uploads/2004/11/22000000/middlebury-general-conduct.pdf.

117   Rice University, *Appropriate Use of Computer Resources*, March 15, 2017, https://d28htnjz2elwuj.cloudfront.net/wp-content/up-loads/2004/11/22000000/middlebury-general-conduct.pdf.

118   Swarthmore College, *Student Code of Conduct: Rules and Regulations*, accessed May 10, 2017, https://d28htnjz2elwuj.cloudfront.net/wp-content/up-loads/2013/10/27202644/swarthmore-code.pdf.

119   Jennifer Kabbany, "Angry mob shuts down Blue Lives Matter speech

Biology Pages, Accessed May 10, 2017, http://www.biology-pages.info/A/AbioticSynthesis.html.

102   Bill Dixon, "Is Life Essentially Different From Inanimate Matter?" *The Richard Dawkins Foundation for Science and Reason*, May 24, 2014, https://richarddawkins.net/2014/05/is-life-essentially-different-from-inanimate-matter/.

103   Richard Gray, "Are we all ALIENS? Support grows for the panspermia theory that claims life on Earth may have arrived here from outer space," *Daily Mail*, August 11, 2015, http://www.dailymail.co.uk/sciencetech/article-3193585/Are-ALIENS-Growing-support-panspermia-theory-life-Earth-carried-outer-space.html.

104   Michaelian, K.: "Thermodynamic dissipation theory for the origin of life," 2011, *Earth System Dynamics*, 2, 37-51, doi:10.5194/esd-2-37-2011, 2011.

105   Schenck v. United States, 249 U.S. 47 (1919).

106   Chaplinsky v. New Hampshire, 315 U.S. 568 (1942).

107   American Civil Liberties Union, *Freedom of Expression* (position paper), accessed May 10, 2017, https://www.aclu.org/other/freedom-expression-aclu-position-paper.

108   "What Are Speech Codes?" *The Foundation for Individual Rights in Education*, accessed May 10, 2017, https://www.thefire.org/spotlight/what-are-speech-codes/.

109   Boston University, *University Conditions of Use & Policy on Computing Ethics*, May 9, 2017, https://d28htnjz2elwuj.cloudfront.net/wp-content/uploads/2005/03/23160000/University-Conditions-of-Use-Policy-on-Computing-Ethics-%C2%BB-Dean-of-Students-_-Boston-University.pdf.

110   Chicago State University, *CSU Computer Usage Policy*, August 22, 2016, https://d28htnjz2elwuj.cloudfront.net/wp-content/up-

at Claremont McKenna College," *The College Fix*, April 7, 2017, https://www.thecollegefix.com/post/32050/.

120   Matthew Reade, "Students Demand Administrators 'Take Action' Against Conservative Journalists," *Claremont Independent*, April 17, 2017, http://claremontindependent.com/students-demand-administrators-take-action-against-conservative-journalists/.

121   "Wellesley Statement from CERE faculty re: Laura Kipnis Freedom Project visit and aftermath," *Foundation for Individual Rights in Education*, March 20, 2017, https://www.thefire.org/subject-facstaffdiscuss-statement-cere-faculty-re-laura-kipnis-freedom-project-visit-aftermath/.

122   Toni Airaksinen, "Anti-rape activists 'shut down' female professor who decried 'sexual paranoia' on campus," *The College Fix*, March 10, 2017, https://www.thecollegefix.com/post/31597/.

123   Jeannie Suk Gersen, "The Trouble With Teaching Rape Law," *The New Yorker*, December 15, 2014, http://www.newyorker.com/news/news-desk/trouble-teaching-rape-law.

124   Erica L. Green, "Bethune-Cookman Graduates Greet Betsy DeVos With Turned Backs," *The New York Times*, May 10, 2017, https://www.nytimes.com/2017/05/10/us/politics/betsy-devos-bethune-cookman-commencement.html.